The Small but Essential Handbook of
Basic Bankruptcy Law

Argentum fugit

Thomas W. Coffey
Scott J. Kelly
Krista L. Kaleps

Tucker Ellis & West LLP
Cleveland, Ohio
2005

Copyright 2005 by Lawriter Corporation
Cincinnati, Ohio

First Edition

For access to federal and more than 20 state law libraries

VISIT OUR WEBSITE
www.casemaker.us

The Casemaker™ Online database is a compilation exclusively owned by Lawriter Corporation and is available to lawyers belonging to a Casemaker Consortium bar association. The database is provided for use under the terms, notices, and conditions as expressly stated under the online end user license agreement to which all users assent in order to access the database.

If you have questions about Casemaker,
please contact your bar association.

ISBN 0-9766565-2-3

Table of Contents

1. Bankruptcy in a Thimble 1
2. Different Chapters of the Bankruptcy Code Explained 3
3. The Discharge of Debt 8
4. The Automatic Stay 10
5. Avoidance of Liens 12
6. The Concept of Exemptions 14
7. Reaffirmation of Debts 17
8. Retirement Plans 19
9. Proofs of Claim and Bar Dates 21
10. Schedules of Debts and Assets 23
11. Meeting of Creditors 25
12. Bankruptcy Depositions (2004 Exams) 27
13. Preferences 29
14. Fraudulent Conveyances 31
15. The Creditors Committee 34
16. Sales of Assets 37
17. Reorganization Financing 39
18. Leases and Contracts 41
19. Fees and Fee Applications 44
20. Plans of Reorganization 47
21. Adversary Proceedings 50
22. Compromises of Claims 52
23. Involuntary Bankruptcy Cases 54
24. Bankruptcy Reform Act of 2005 56
25. One Dozen Critical Pitfalls in Chapter 7 Consumer Cases 66
26. Ten Critical Questions to Answer Before Filing a Personal Bankruptcy Case 78
27. Ten Critical Questions to Answer Before Filing a Chapter 11 Business Reorganization Case 87

Preface

This little book is designed to provide an easily readable overview of the vast landscape of bankruptcy law. The focus here is on the big picture, and the goal is to put the separate parts of the law into context. Those looking for detailed explanations of these concepts must find them elsewhere.

The authors are attorneys who practice bankruptcy law. We believe that this book will be useful for attorneys who are not bankruptcy specialists. In addition, we think that it will be a good source for business managers, students, and professionals who need some familiarity with the concepts discussed. Law libraries are amply stocked with scholarly and authoritative texts used by bankruptcy lawyers. Our purpose here is different and we make no effort to write here for our fellow specialists.

We know that some who read this book will be considering filing for bankruptcy relief. For this audience, we advise the selection of an experienced lawyer with whom you are comfortable. Bankruptcy can bring desperately needed relief. But it is a complicated part of the law and it is no place to venture without an experienced lawyer to protect your interests.

We feel honored to practice in an area of law that particularly values fairness and equity. A myriad of personal or business circumstances can cause people of all walks of life, as well as business entities, to need a fresh start. The availability of this relief is a critical part of a vital and vigorous national economy. We hope that our book advances the general understanding of this complicated and intricate subject.

About the Authors

Thomas W. Coffey heads the bankruptcy practice group at Tucker Ellis & West LLP. Based in the firm's Cleveland headquarters, Mr. Coffey leads an integrated practice concentrated in both Chapter 11 reorganization and corporate finance law. He served as an adjunct faculty member at his alma mater, the University of Cincinnati College of Law, winning the Adjunct Faculty Teaching Excellence Award in 2001. Mr. Coffey was a member of the panel of Chapter 7 bankruptcy trustees in Cincinnati and currently practices in Chapter 11 proceedings throughout the midwestern and eastern United States.

Scott J. Kelly is a trial lawyer with significant experience in Chapter 11 bankruptcy matters. Admitted in California as well as Ohio, Mr. Kelly has appeared on behalf of various clients in bankruptcy cases in Delaware, New York, Ohio, Kentucky, California, and Missouri. Mr. Kelly concentrates his practice on the litigation aspects of corporate reorganization cases and has substantial experience in asbestos litigation, as well as preference litigation and challenges to Chapter 11 plans of reorganization.

Krista L. Kaleps is an associate in the Cleveland office of Tucker Ellis & West LLP. She has substantial experience in Chapter 11 litigation and related commercial litigation matters. Ms. Kaleps was managing editor of the *Journal of Law and Health* at Cleveland Marshall School of Law, and attended the St. Petersburg Summer Law Institute at St. Petersburg, Russia.

PUBLISHER'S NOTE

The Small but Essential Handbook of Basic Bankruptcy Law has been published in two forms, the Standard Edition and the Lawyer's Edition.

The Standard Edition (98 pages, $14.95) contains text strictly generated by Coffey, Kelly, and Kaleps. It was written with the general public in mind.

The Lawyer's Edition (274 pages, $24.95) contains the above-mentioned text, but it also provides non-bankruptcy attorneys with selected bankruptcy statutes, rules, and case law. Many chapter headings in the text contain references to sections of the U.S. Bankruptcy Code or to the Federal Rules of Bankruptcy Procedure. Most of these cited materials are included in the Lawyer's Edition. Additionally, we have provided website addresses, links and other information applicable to federal bankruptcy courts.

Readers of the Standard Edition who desire a single book with the statutes, rules, and case law available may wish to purchase the Lawyer's Edition as well.

Both editions are available at **www.casemaker.cc**

Acknowledgements

The partners of Tucker Ellis & West LLP set out in July of 2003 to create "a different kind of law firm." They were committed to creating a firm in which success would be measured by mastery of the law, creative approaches to complex problems, and the achievement of remarkable results for clients. The traditional billable hour metrics were to play no part in this system.

The result was the creation of an institution where scholarship flourishes, creativity thrives, and collegiality breeds teamwork. The authors of this book are privileged to be part of Tucker Ellis & West LLP. We are grateful to our colleagues for the opportunity to research and write this book. We are particularly grateful for the opportunity to carry the ball for our clients when the legal issues involve insolvency.

The authors are proud to acknowledge the superior efforts of our legal secretary, Kellie M. Cain, through whose talented hands all of the words in this book passed. Finally, a tip of our collective hat is in order for our patient and perseverant editors, Craig Slanker and Karen Gossage of Casemaker Print Publishing, and for Casemaker's Joseph W. Shea III, whose gentle (and not so gentle) nudges propelled us onward toward success.

Thomas W. Coffey
Scott J. Kelly
Krista L. Kaleps
Cleveland, Ohio 2005

Chapter 1: Bankruptcy in a Thimble

When the giant roulette wheel on the nationally televised program "Wheel of Fortune" lands on the space marked "Bankrupt," an audible sigh of dismay usually emanates from the audience. "Bankrupt," in that limited game show context, means loss of everything gained so far. In real life, the sighs that accompany a bankruptcy filing are often sighs of relief. Many individual debtors are overborne by indebtedness and frequently by problems ranging from job loss to divorce to uninsured illness or injury. For these individuals, the filing of the petition, along with the automatic order of the federal court halting collection activities, signals the beginning of a welcome opportunity to start over.

Bankruptcy is a federal remedy for otherwise intractable problems brought about by insolvency or the inability to pay debts as they come due. Interestingly enough, insolvency is not a prerequisite to the voluntary case. However, in a contested involuntary case, the petitioners must still prove that the debtor is not paying debts as they become due. Bankruptcy is exclusively federal; the U.S. Constitution empowers Congress to enact uniform laws for the administration of bankruptcy cases.

Bankruptcy is intended to provide relief to debtors primarily through the discharge, which is an order of the Federal Court prohibiting any action to collect on all or part of the indebtedness of the debtor. Bankruptcy is also intended to treat creditors fairly in the process, and to treat similarly situated creditors equally.

Bankruptcy is a critical part of a capitalist economic system. Without it, business risks would be unmanageable, because debt and debtors' prison would dog the honest but unlucky entrepreneur until death finally brought relief. In some societies without the concept of bankruptcy, families were hounded for money even after the death of a hapless merchant. In at least one otherwise modern and thriving economy, it was common and expected, until recently, for the CEO of an insolvent business to literally commit suicide by falling on a sword.

Our system is meant to encourage bold and sometimes risky vision. The fresh ideas that create new jobs, new classes of wealth, and in some cases, entirely new economic realities, often result in failure. Examples of highly successful and motivated individuals who have availed themselves of bankruptcy relief include silver trader Nelson Bunker Hunt, real estate magnate Donald Trump, and even film actress Kim Basinger. Ms. Basinger lost a large verdict in a breach of contract suit after her refusal to play a role she found too gruesome. She decided that her best course of action was to file for bankruptcy.

Bankruptcy is considered a collective remedy for both the debtor and all creditors. Bankruptcy cases, once filed, cannot be dismissed by the filer without the permission of the court. For this reason, the planning process prior to filing is usually the most important part of the case for the debtor or the petitioning creditors. The creation of contingency plans tends to minimize risks and maximize results in the courtroom, where flexibility is critical and the initial plan is often met with unexpected obstacles.

Chapter 2: Different Chapters of the Bankruptcy Code Explained

Bankruptcy is organized into Chapters of the Bankruptcy Code, which is found in Title 11 of the U.S. Code. The Chapters are structured to provide different kinds of cases for differently situated debtors. Here are the most commonly cited chapters:

Chapter 7—Liquidation—Chapter 7 is the "basic" bankruptcy chapter. It is available to all debtors, except some middle-class filers who will be forced to use Chapter 13 under the 2005 Reform Act. In Chapter 7, a trustee "liquidates" (usually by selling it) all non-exempt property which is not subject to liens, and pays the proceeds to creditors as a dividend. In most consumer cases, there is, in fact, no non-exempt property which is not already subject to liens, and no property is administered. These cases are closed as "no asset" cases. All of the debts of the individual debtor are usually discharged. Business entities (corporations, partnerships, LLCs) do not get a discharge and must cease operations. The liened property may be returned or kept by the individual debtor, at the debtor's option. But if the debtor elects to keep the property, the debtor must pay off the liens, sometimes at a reduced amount.

Chapter 9—Adjustment of Debts of a Municipality— This chapter is limited to cases involving municipalities, or municipally chartered institutions such as public school districts, municipal hospitals, or other municipal subdivisions. Most often these cases require negotiations with creditors

Different Chapters of the Bankruptcy Code Explained

prior to filing and often involve adjustments to the municipal bond portfolios of the debtor.

Probably the best-known case of this kind involved Orange County, California. Speculation in the financial derivatives market caused the county to suddenly lose millions of dollars. A Chapter 9 petition was filed to stop the county from losing all of its operating cash to creditors. This action was very successful. The finances were stabilized through the issuance of strong municipal bonds and a reorganization plan, which structured the debts into manageable payments, was put into place.

In contrast, an attempt by Bridgeport, Connecticut to restructure under Chapter 9 was unsuccessful. Following the Bridgeport case, the law was amended to make clear that states have the power to deny municipalities the authorization to file for bankruptcy relief. Such authorization is required before municipalities can reorganize their finances in bankruptcy court. Chapter 9 is highly specialized relief under the bankruptcy code and is almost never used. It is easily the least-used chapter of the Bankruptcy Code.

Chapter 11—Reorganization—Chapter 11 cases are available to individuals, but are rarely used by them. Chapter 11 filings are overwhelmingly corporate in nature. Some of America's most important industrial entities, including most of the steel manufacturers, most of the airlines, and a large variety of other "household name" corporations, have at one time reorganized under Chapter 11.

Every year, hundreds of businesses are saved from extinction through Chapter 11 reorganizations. A successful reorganization allows creditors to be paid more than they would receive if the company were liquidated. It also preserves jobs, and often, the company itself. In reorganization cases, some debt is paid by the debtor, usually over time, and the remainder is discharged.

Most of the large cases involve substantial changes in corporate structure. Corporate restructuring often includes the sale of most (or even all) assets, infusions of new equity or debt financing, and dilution or elimination of entire classes of equity. A strong recent trend involves the discharge of corporate liabilities to pensioners, with the federal Pension Benefit Guarantee Corporation often left to pay sharply reduced benefits to pension creditors.

Chapter 12—Adjustment of the Debts of a Family Farmer—Chapter 12 is designed to keep family owned farms in the hands of the families who own them. Its flexible reorganization plan process focuses on the cure, waiver, or elimination of defaults which would otherwise result in foreclosure on the farm real estate or personal property. This streamlined form of reorganization requires a plan to be filed within 90 days of the petition. It also requires the trustee to be assigned a substantial income from farm operations to effectuate the terms of the plan. It is used most often in the western agricultural states.

Chapter 13—Adjustment of Debts of an Individual with Regular Income—Chapter 13 cases are often called "wage earner cases." This chapter involves reorganization through a fairly standardized plan of reorganization which is confirmed without the vote of creditors. Under these plans, an automatic payroll deduction transfers a portion of the debtor's income on a monthly or weekly basis to a standing Chapter 13 trustee. The trustee generally presides over a fairly sophisticated operation which collects the wage deductions from thousands of Chapter 13 debtors. The trustee then distributes the withheld wages on a periodic basis, usually monthly. The creditors' remuneration is in accordance with the Chapter 13 Plan filed by each debtor and confirmed by the court.

Under the Reform Act of 2005, a substantial number of middle-class debtors will be required to file under Chapter 13 instead of Chapter 7. Both of these chapters (and all of the other chapters) are based on the bankruptcy discharge. The primary difference is that Chapter 7 generally provides a complete discharge, while the Chapter 13 discharge is partial in nature. The discharge of the debt is granted only in return for the repayment of the other portion of the indebtedness through payments under Chapter 13.

Historically, many Chapter 13 cases have failed because debtors cannot function for long periods of time (three to five years) while absorbing the payroll deduction for prepetition debt. It is not clear how failed Chapter 13 cases, which would have previously been converted to Chapter 7 liquidation, will be treated under the Reform Act of 2005.

General Provisions and Rules

Chapters 1, 3, and 5 of the Bankruptcy Code contain general provisions that are applicable in all chapters. These provisions create the role of the trustee, set forth the filing requirements, provide for the avoidance of certain transfers, and establish the automatic stay. They also govern the use of property of the estate and the debtor's ability to conduct business during bankruptcy.

There are nine separate groups of rules of bankruptcy procedure, currently ending with Rule 9036. However, these are organized into nine related "parts," which are not numbered sequentially. Even the erudite members of the bankruptcy bar do not have to cope (yet) with nine thousand rules!

Chapter 3: The Discharge of Debt
[Sections 523, 524 & 727]

The discharge of debt is the foundation of all bankruptcy law. A discharge is an order issued by the federal court, providing that certain debts are totally or partially cancelled, or "discharged" by operation of law. In most liquidation cases (Chapter 7 of the Bankruptcy Code) involving individual, non-corporate debtors, the discharge wipes away all debt incurred before the case. There are certain exceptions to discharge (see Section 523) but they are difficult for creditors to implement and are rarely used. Non-individual debtors (corporations, partnerships, LLCs, etc.) do not get a discharge in a liquidation case. Instead, they stop operating and eventually cease to exist.

Some debts are non-dischargeable, including domestic support obligations, educational loans, loan repayments to retirement plans, and debts for restitution ordered by courts, or debts based on willful and malicious injury to others. Theft, embezzlement, larceny and similar behaviors, as well as debts based on accidents caused by drunk drivers, are also non-dischargeable.

Under the 2005 Reform Act, consumer debts for "luxury goods" incurred within 90 days of filing the Chapter 7 petition are non-dischargeable. In addition, debts for "cash advances" taken within 70 days of filing are also non-dischargeable.

The 2005 Reform Act consistently makes it more difficult for consumers to discharge all of their debt. Some consumer debt was not dischargeable before the Reform Act. The

Reform Act addresses non-dischargeable consumer debt by broadening the scope of "luxury goods" and reducing the threshold amount of an offending "cash advance." It also increases the time period prior to the petition date in which such transactions can be scrutinized.

In reorganization cases under Chapters 11, 12, and 13, the debtor usually pays back a portion of indebtedness under a plan of reorganization, and the remainder is discharged. This use of partial discharge is the magic fuel of reorganization. The theory is that everyone benefits from the debtor making some payments, even if it is not the full amount. This concept is so powerful that creditors' lobbies successfully convinced Congress to require it of certain middle-class consumer debtors.

Once a discharge is issued, a creditor who attempts to collect discharged debts faces severe penalties. Any collection activities are treated as contempt of the federal court. To protect debtors and ensure the integrity of the process, the courts zealously guard the sanctity of the discharge. For this reason, the discharge is taken seriously by creditors, and violations are relatively uncommon.

Chapter 4: The Automatic Stay
[Section 362]

The automatic stay is an Order of the Bankruptcy Court which strictly forbids any and all collection activities from the minute (literally) that the bankruptcy case is filed. This has the effect of "freezing" the debtor's assets in place until the parties and the court can decide who (if anyone) will be paid on claims and who may be entitled to seize liened property. The idea is to distribute the debtor's money and property only according to priorities established by bankruptcy law and eliminate the concept of the race to the courthouse. The automatic stay remains in effect until it is replaced by the discharge (see the previous chapter) in a successful case, or is dissolved by the dismissal of an unsuccessful case.

The automatic stay and the related concept of property of the estate (Section 541 of the Bankruptcy Code) are very broad and are strictly enforced by the courts. For example, in the case of *United States v. Whiting Pools, Inc.*, 462 U.S. 198 (1983), the court ordered the IRS to return money which was seized in a tax levy prior to the filing of the case. The Bankruptcy Code provides procedures for relief from the stay and they must be followed before proceeding against the debtors or liened property.

A critical function of the automatic stay is to prevent creditors from disrupting the business of the reorganizing debtor (or the life of an individual debtor) by seizing property under state law remedies. Separate parts of the code allow debtors to assume leases or contracts by continuing to make payments so they may keep the property. Other sections allow business debtors to use liened property or borrowed money and its cash flow proceeds to continue in business.

Creditors are certainly entitled to their say on such matters, and the right to obtain relief from the automatic stay is a due process issue. However, creditors must proceed only through the court, which acts as a central clearinghouse for property rights of the debtor and creditors. In reorganization cases, creditors may be forced to forego rights to seize property needed for the reorganization. In individual cases, creditors with liens may see parts of their claims discharged, to the extent the claim exceeds the value of collateral securing the debt.

Sometimes these issues affect parties other than the debtor or the creditor seeking relief. For example, a secured creditor's state law right to collect on accounts, if unfettered, could easily put a reorganizing debtor out of business. This collection could foreclose any chance of recovery for unsecured creditors. The court, if it finds that the secured creditor is not at risk of diminishing returns, may delay such actions to allow a reorganization plan to be confirmed. In effect, the provisions of the code allow the court the discretion to permit continued operations while the debtor reorganizes, even though it greatly inconveniences one or more secured creditors. These provisions allow the debtor and the unsecured creditors to have a better chance of rehabilitation and repayment.

Chapter 5: Avoidance of Liens
[Sections 544 & 545]

A lien is a limited ownership interest in real or personal property. As such, it is considered property itself and its owner cannot be deprived of it without due process of law.

Due process, in the bankruptcy context, includes avoidance of the lien if it is improperly perfected. Avoidance means that the lien is declared invalid, leaving the creditor with a claim that is unsecured instead of secured. This result can occur as a consequence of the creditor:

- failing to file a mortgage, financing statements, or mechanics lien notices;
- filing in the wrong office or not all required offices;
- filing improperly signed or drafted documents; or
- failing to file notarized documents where required, in some cases.

Avoidance is accomplished by the filing of a complaint seeking a court order invalidating a lien. The creditor has 30 days from service of the complaint to file an answer. The resulting case takes place within the bankruptcy case, is tried in the bankruptcy court, and is called an adversary proceeding. State law usually governs because Section 544 (often called the strong-arm clause) puts the trustee or debtor-in-possession in the position of a properly perfected lien creditor. The priority battle then plays out between the properly perfected creditor and the defendant under principles of state law.

These cases are often very defensible on the law and the facts, and many of them are settled. However, prompt action is important to avoid a default judgment.

Related provisions of the code permit individual debtors to redeem liened property by paying only the value of the collateral and discharging the debt above this value. One interesting use of the provisions of the code relating to liens allows reorganizing debtors to lower the interest rate on certain secured liens to a market rate of interest. These market rates may be several points lower than the contract rate.

Chapter 6: The Concept of Exemptions
[Section 522; ORC § 2329.66]

Exemptions are statutory provisions placing all or part of certain property of the estate out of reach of the trustee for liquidation purposes. The concept exists only in Chapter 7 liquidation cases and only to individual (natural person) debtors. Corporate debtors do not get the benefit of exemptions.

Ohio and many other states opted out of the exemptions provided by Bankruptcy Code Section 522. The Bankruptcy Code allowed states to opt out of the federal system of exemptions as a political compromise in 1978 to obtain passage of the bill. Consequently, a state law system of exemptions, ORC[1] § 2329.66, applies in bankruptcy cases and also applies outside the bankruptcy context in Ohio.

California has also opted out of the Section 522 exemptions. In California, debtors have the option of choosing from two exemption schemes. One scheme virtually tracks Section 522 and essentially gives debtors the ability to use the code exemptions. Alternatively, debtors can use California's general exemptions. These exemptions are much more liberal and allow debtors to keep more than they would under the Bankruptcy Code's exemptions. For example, depending on factors such as age and marital status, Californians can take between $50,000 and $150,000 for the homestead exemption. California also allows debtors to exempt all of their household appliances, clothing, furnishings, and personal effects. But this allowance only applies if the items are ordinarily and reasonably necessary for use by the debtor and family at the principal dwelling, and as long as they are not extraordinarily valuable.

---
[1] Ohio Revised Code

In contrast, the Bankruptcy Code's homestead exemption is only $17,425 and the exemption for household goods/clothing/etc. is limited to $450 per item and an aggregate of $9,300. In Ohio, the homestead exemption is $5,000. Ohio also allows exemptions for household goods, clothing, etc., but incorporates relatively low limits on each item and the aggregate amount exempted, making the exemption less generous from the debtor's perspective.

The 2005 Reform Act imposes a residency requirement (ranging from 180 to 730 days) upon debtors seeking to utilize state exemptions not otherwise offered under the federal scheme. The residency requirement discourages debtors from making a pre-bankruptcy move to another state to obtain favorable exemptions. Under the provision permitting states to "opt out" of the federal exemption scheme, there is no uniform national law of exemptions.

To make sense, the exemptions must be considered with liens. For example, a married couple living in Ohio and owning a house worth $160,000 with a mortgage balance of $130,000 might well keep the house in a Chapter 7 case under the following analysis:

Fair Market Value:	$160,000
Mortgage:	$130,000
Real Estate Commission	$11,200
Costs of Sale:	$2,500
Husband's Homestead Exemption: (ORC § 2329.66(A)(1))	$5,000
Wife's Homestead Exemption: (ORC § 2329.66(A)(1))	$5,000
Husband's Exemption: (ORC § 2329.66(A)(18))	$400
Wife's Exemption: (ORC § 2329.66(A)(18))	$400
Equity:	**$5,500**

The Concept of Exemptions

Depending on the amount of debt to be satisfied, the trustee might abandon the house, meaning that the debtors could keep it if they reaffirmed the mortgage debt. Alternatively, the trustee might allow the debtors to borrow $5,500 from family members to buy out the equity, which would still allow them to keep the house. In a case with total unsecured debt of $150,000, the trustee might abandon the equity and close the case without pursuing it. If the debtors owed only $10,000 to unsecured creditors, the trustee might be much more inclined to collect and administer the equity, because it would pay a far higher percentage of total claims. Other factors, such as the likelihood that the entire estate would have to be paid to tax creditors, meaning no distribution for general unsecured creditors, might also cause the trustee to close the case without pursuing the equity.

It is not unusual for Chapter 7 debtors to retain homes or cars even after filing for bankruptcy relief. The trustee views these assets from the standpoint of unsecured creditors. If the assets are leased or fully liened, the liquidation sale of them would yield nothing for the estate and the trustee will ignore them. Some people have difficulty understanding this result. It is easy to grasp, however, when viewed from the perspective of whether unsecured creditors will benefit from the sale of assets. Bankruptcy is not designed to be punitive.

Some states, such as Florida, provide very generous homestead exemptions. State law is relevant to the analysis of exemptions in all states which have opted out of the federal exemptions provided by Section 522. Consultation with a lawyer actually practicing in such states is almost mandatory for correct results. Often state codes include provisions related to exemptions in parts of the state statute not dealing directly with exemptions.

Chapter 7: Reaffirmation of Debts
[Section 524(c)]

Debtors are permitted to agree to pay a debt after the discharge is granted. Usually, this applies to individuals who want to keep liened property. They agree to pay the debt, or perhaps a portion of the debt, and the creditor allows them to keep the property.

This procedure invites abuse from unscrupulous creditors, particularly those who seek reaffirmation of unsecured debts, which would benefit only the creditor. Consequently, the code provides that a reaffirmation agreement is effective only if the agreement is made prior to discharge and is filed with the court. Such agreements must:

(1) contain a clear and conspicuous statement advising the debtor that the agreement may be rescinded at any time prior to discharge or within 60 days after filing with the court, whichever is later;

(2) contain a clear and conspicuous statement that reaffirmation is not required; and

(3) be accompanied by the declaration or affidavit of the debtor's attorney that the agreement does not impose an undue hardship.

Additional requirements were created by the 2005 Reform Act. If the debtor is not represented by counsel, the debtor must be provided with a long list of disclosures before signing the reaffirmation agreement.

Reaffirmation agreements are time-sensitive. If they are not filed prior to discharge, it becomes too late to bind the debtor. The code provides that a debtor may pay any debt after discharge. But it is necessary to file the agreement in a timely fashion under Section 524 in order to make the obligation binding.

Chapter 8: Retirement Plans

The enactment of the 2005 Reform Act has codified certain U.S. Supreme Court cases holding most retirement plans beyond the reach of creditors. The act imposes a one million dollar limit on the exemption of such assets from estates, but resolves the question of whether such assets are protected in favor of the debtor. The one million dollar cap is capable of being increased in certain circumstances by order of court.

Whether creditors can acquire assets inside a debtor's retirement plan in bankruptcy proceedings has provided fertile ground for litigation, with mixed results. In 1992, in the case of *Patterson v. Shumate*, 504 U.S. 758 (1992) the U.S. Supreme Court ruled that 401(k) retirement plan assets are excluded from bankruptcy estates because the anti-alienation provisions of ERISA render them similar to trust assets. The ruling was significant, in particular, because it applied in every state, regardless of whether a particular state had opted out of the federal exemptions. Under *Patterson v. Shumate*, 401(k) assets were deemed excluded, not exempted, making the various exemption schemes irrelevant.

In 2005, the Supreme Court followed the *Patterson v. Shumate* holding with a ruling that IRAs were similar to 401(k) plans, and are therefore exempt under Section 522. The case of *Rousey v. Jacoway*, 125 S.Ct. 1561 (2005), may be less sweeping in the scope of its ruling than *Patterson v. Shumate*, because it may be binding only in states which have adopted Section 522's exemption scheme.

This left open, prior to the enactment of the Reform Act, the question of whether IRAs would always be exempt in a state opting out of Section 522. Many states exempt IRAs and similar plans "to the extent reasonably necessary for the support of the debtor and his dependants." Some draconian cases have divested debtors of portions of even small plans under this language. On the other hand, this same language is included in the federal exemptions, but was not at issue in the *Rousey* case.

Important social policies are implicated in both Supreme Court decisions. The court has discerned Congressional intent to protect retirement assets as if they are held by someone else for the debtor's retirement, instead of being owned by the debtor and therefore at risk prior to retirement. This interpretation recognizes that it is desirable to allow people to plan for their own future and save their own funds for retirement, instead of becoming dependant on public support. Protection of the retirement funds is required during bankruptcy if the savings are to be effective and encouraged. Nearly all of the recent holdings have trended toward protecting retirement assets.

The 2005 Reform Act will affect debtors who engage in pre-bankruptcy retirement planning. The Reform Act limits the amount of tax-exempt savings that can be exempted from the bankruptcy estate to an aggregate of $1 million. (See Sections 522(b)(3)(C), (b)(4), (d)(12), (n) of the Federal Bankruptcy Code). In addition, if a Chapter 11 debtor modifies its retiree benefits plan within 180 days before filing for bankruptcy, and it is established that it was insolvent when it made the modification, the court may reinstate the benefits and unwind the modification.

Chapter 9: Proofs of Claim and Bar Dates
[Section 502]

A proof of claim is a simple (currently one page) form which is submitted by a creditor to the court, itemizing what is due. Almost all of them are filed with attachments. The trustee uses the proofs of claim to see how much money is due to creditors and how the estate should be divided among them. For years, case law was exceptionally severe in its treatment of late claims. Because of the importance of these documents in calculating distributions, everyone who missed the bar date (the last day to file a timely proof of claim) was barred from any recovery from the estate, nearly without exception.

Current case law allows late filed proofs of claim under some circumstances. For every creditor and every lawyer representing creditors, the best course of action is to file a claim at the earliest notice of the case.

Many case notices now say not to file claims because no assets are discovered yet. However, it is usually better to file anyway, to minimize the risk of missing the bar date later. Even if the bar date has passed, a claim should still be filed. Under current Supreme Court holdings, a motion to allow the late proof now has a reasonable opportunity of being granted.

Filing the claim is free—there are no fees. Computing the amount due is often the most complicated part of preparing the claim. Claims can be amended after filing if the amount due or other details change. It does not cost very much money for attorneys to assist with the filing of the claim, except in very complicated cases where the fee is usually a very good investment anyway.

Claims can be assigned (sold) to buyers during a case. There is a booming business in trading claims in large Chapter 11 cases. Some solicitations to buy are deliberately structured to look like communications from the court. In many cases, the offer to buy comes from an investment bank with inside information, and these offers are rarely good for the seller.

In some reorganization cases, a non-filing claimant may still be paid a dividend based on the amount scheduled by the debtor for that claimant. However, it is still the best practice to file a proof of claim to avoid having the claim cancelled or amended downward after the bar date. Proofs of claim also indicate the nature of the claim: secured, unsecured, priority, etc. In many cases, it is advisable to file two or more separate proofs of claim to properly reflect the status of each part of the claim.

Priority unsecured claims are paid in full by trustees before any distribution is made on general unsecured claims. And, if claims are secured by a lien on property, those secured claims are paid before either priority unsecured or general unsecured claims. Priority unsecured claims include claims for domestic support obligations; claims of employees for wages, claims on commissions, or benefits; claims of customers to recover deposits on goods for sale, and tax claims. In addition, expenses of the trustee and lawyers handling the case are accorded a high priority.

Chapter 10: Schedules of Debts and Assets
[Section 521]

A bankruptcy petition initiates a case. A debtor must file schedules of debts and assets either with the petition or immediately thereafter. In the case of an individual (natural person) debtor, a schedule of exempt property must also be filed. In addition, all debtors must file a statement of financial affairs. The 2005 Reform Act requires debtors to disclose the value, operations, and profitability of entities of which the debtor owns or has a controlling or "substantial" interest.

These documents must be filed on prescribed official forms. All filings must be electronic. It is no longer acceptable to make a paper filing with the clerk, except for a proof of claim. The required filings are not very complicated for attorneys, but many consumers or small business filers find them overwhelming. In some cases under the new provisions of the 2005 Reform Act, attorneys may be liable if the debtor supplies misleading information in the schedules. Some commentators are even opining that attorneys must now visit consumer debtors at home to ensure that the schedules match the property on hand.

Business cases pose their own challenges concerning scheduling claims and assets. It is strange but true that a case the size of Kmart or Enron is filed on the same forms as a consumer case. With special permission, some "shortcuts" are allowed in such cases to keep the task of scheduling all the inventory from overwhelming the case. However, courts and the offices of the U.S. Trustee generally take a hard line on the standards of accuracy and completeness required in

Schedules of Debts and Assets

these documents. More importantly, attention to detail on the part of the debtor and counsel for the debtor are required and rewarded in the context of these schedules.

It has become increasingly common for creditors to claim that fraud, as opposed to financial exigency, motivates debtors. This is rarely true, but sloppy schedules generate arguments that:

- property is deliberately omitted or undervalued to deprive creditors of fair recovery;

- creditors are omitted or scheduled with wrong addresses to deprive them of notice and the right to be heard;

- statements of financial affairs or monthly operating reports fail to include details showing that reorganization is not feasible; and

- the debtor's inattention to detail is proof of incompetence, inability to reorganize, or fraud that vitiates the entitlement to a discharge.

Production of correct, accurate and complete schedules eliminates these arguments.

On the other hand, some debtors do try to cut corners. Leaving a boat, plane, car or house off the asset schedules, failing to note a recent gift to a relative on the statement of financial affairs, or similar "mistakes" can be evidence of fraudulent intent. Courts do not hesitate to withhold the discharge as a penalty in such cases.

Chapter 11: Meeting of Creditors
[Section 341]

Every bankruptcy case generates a notice of the filing, which is mailed by the court to all creditors. That notice, or a subsequent notice, informs creditors that a meeting of creditors will be held at which the trustee will preside, and the debtor will be examined under oath. This meeting is required under Section 341 and is commonly called the "341 Meeting."

It is common for creditors to assume that something important will happen at the 341 Meeting. In consumer cases, it almost never does. In most jurisdictions, these are scheduled at 7½ minute (!) increments, and a bored trustee presides over a small crowd by repeating a few rudimentary questions. It is nearly always a waste of time for creditors to attend, because the duration of the meeting is too limited, the docket runs late, and the format is wrong for serious questions. However, the 341 Meeting is a statutory requirement, and it is critical that debtors attend and give appropriate answers to the questions propounded by the trustee.

In business reorganization cases, the U.S. Trustee presides over the 341 Meeting. These meetings last longer and can be productive. In general, executive officers and financial officers are sworn in, and questions draw reasonably well-prepared answers. More importantly, in smaller cases, the Creditors Committee may be formed in conjunction with this meeting. In larger Chapter 11 cases, the Creditors Committee is usually formed right away and it is typically dominated by creditors with exceptionally large claims. However, the

Meeting of Creditors

2005 Reform Act includes provisions which may result in some creditors with smaller claims also having a seat on the committee.

Under the Reform Act, if the debtor files a prepackaged plan, the Court may dispense with the 341 Meeting of creditors altogether. [See Section 341(e)]. The debtor can prepare a prepackaged plan before filing for bankruptcy. This procedure is used exclusively in Chapter 11 cases and circumvents some of the requirements for solicitation of votes of the plan. It is rarely used.

In general, no creditor should make serious scheduling sacrifices to attend a 341 Meeting, especially without counsel. While it is sometimes possible to pick up some useful information there (usually from discussions in the hallway, not inside), it is not possible to increase the chances of getting paid. Creditors with serious issues are better off spending their time and money with counsel, finding a way to further their cause in court. And it is possible (and usually cheaper, in terms of time) to obtain information directly from debtor's counsel instead of attending the meeting of creditors.

Creditors are sometimes surprised to see no judge at the 341 Meeting. In fact, the statute prohibits the judge from attending any meeting of creditors. A major part of the job description of bankruptcy trustees involves presiding at meetings of creditors. Perhaps these meetings will one day be eliminated by statute, because they are so nonproductive. Until statutory changes are made, however, debtors should view the 341 Meeting as their best chance to impress the trustee by being cooperative and informative.

Chapter 12: Bankruptcy Depositions
(2004 Exams), Rule 2004

Bankruptcy, like nearly every other advanced field of human endeavor, comes with its own jargon. Three prominent examples are numerical in nature: the 341 Meeting (see Chapter 11); the 9019 Motion (see Chapter 22); and the 2004 Exam.

The 2004 Exam is governed by Bankruptcy Rule 2004. This rule provides for a kind of "super deposition," which is not subject to many of the procedural safeguards found in the rules of civil procedure. It was inevitable that the freewheeling discovery allowed under the rule would be compared to a "fishing expedition," and a number of cases have used that rather shopworn analogy.

The 2004 Exam is derived from common law which allows for the comprehensive examination of debtors to discover fraud, transfers of assets, and the circumstances leading to insolvency. However, the modern 2004 Exam applies not only to debtors, but to any party in interest, including expert witnesses.

2004 Exams are initiated by motions to the court under Rule 2004 and are subject to motions to quash. Debtors (and their officers, in the case of corporate debtors) may be compelled to attend at any location fixed by the court. Other deponents may not usually be required to travel more than 100 miles. Subpoenas may be issued by the court or attorneys on behalf of the court and documents are subject to production.

Bankruptcy cases, particularly reorganization cases, turn on the free flow of information. The rule expressly allows, among many other things,

- questions relating to the operation of reorganizing businesses;
- the desirability of continued operations;
- the source of money or property to be acquired for purposes of consummating a plan; and
- "any other matter relevant to the case or to the formulation of a plan."

Given the breadth of this scope provision, it is very difficult (legally) to restrict or obstruct questioning of a witness.

One of the few sustainable objections relates to the use of 2004 Exams to advance state court litigation. Some courts will not permit the procedure as an end run around state court discovery. A similar theory may restrict use of 2004 Exams where adversary proceedings are pending.

Chapter 13: Preferences
[Section 547]

Preferences are often mentioned with, and are often confused with, fraudulent conveyances. But the meanings of the terms are completely different.

A preference is a payment made by the debtor to a creditor on preexisting, "old" debt (not a C.O.D. or current payment for something new) before the bankruptcy. The "lookback" period is typically is 90 days; it can be longer in some circumstances.

The Bankruptcy Code allows trustees or Debtors in Possession to file a complaint seeking to recover preferential payments from the creditors who received the payments during the "lookback" period prior to the filing of the case. Once a complaint is filed and served, an answer is due within 30 days. In a business case, if the preference claim is worth less than $10,000, the complaint must be filed in the defendant's home jurisdiction. But if the defendant is an insider, the limit drops to $1,000. [See 28 U.S.C. § 1409 (b).]

Preference cases are very defensible (usually) and the great majority are settled for considerably less than the claimed amount. Section 547 provides the "cookbook"; it has a recipe for the case in chief, and another recipe for defenses, prominently including payments (even if late) made in the ordinary course, and credit for new goods and services furnished.

The name "preference" comes from the concept that one creditor should not be "preferred" over another upon

Preferences

insolvency or even prior to the case filing. The law is designed to keep creditors from "dismembering the debtor during his slide into bankruptcy" (according to the legislative history) by demanding, or suing for, past due payments. The "rush to the courthouse" mentality is thus somewhat discouraged by the preference laws, which tend to invalidate judicial liens. Any involuntary "transfer" such as a judicial lien, tax lien, or mechanics lien, even without actual seizure of property, is subject to avoidance as a preference.

However, under the 2005 Reform Act, transfers of less than $5,000 cannot be avoided. In consumer cases, the minimum amount required to file a preference claim is $600. Therefore, the Reform Act should curb the filing of mass-produced nuisance value preference complaints in both business and consumer cases. [See Section 547 (c)(9).]

Defense of preference claims is dominated by the "ordinary course of business" exception to the rule. The most common technique is to prepare an analysis of all invoices and checks issued between the creditor and debtor during the time period at least one year prior to the filing of the petition. If the debtor always paid late (beyond invoice terms) during the course of business relations, the analysis will establish an "ordinary" course of (late) payments which will defeat the preference claim. Amendments to the law provided by the Bankruptcy Reform Act of 2005 purport to allow creditors to rely on the course of business in the industry as a whole or between the parties specifically. This change should further enhance the chances of successfully defending preference claims. [See Section 547 (c)(2).]

Chapter 14: Fraudulent Conveyances
[Section 548]

There are very few parts of the commercial law that are as complicated as fraudulent conveyance law. The term "fraudulent conveyance" is so often linked with the term "preference" (see Chapter 13), that many attorneys confuse the two legal theories.

Both preferences and fraudulent conveyances are subject to avoidance (the judicial unwinding or reversal of the transaction), and both relate to impermissible transfers of the debtor's property prior to the filing of the case. However, the key distinction is that a preference is always a payment for a stale debt, while a fraudulent conveyance, by its very nature, involves a transfer of property for no consideration, or less than fair consideration. These requirements allow for very little overlap between the two doctrines.

All states have statutes, derived from the English Statute of Elizabeth (1571) which prohibit transfers made to hinder, delay, or defraud creditors, or transactions made for less than fair consideration. These statutes generally apply to the period four to six years after the transfer, and are available to the trustee or debtor in possession under Section 544 (the strong-arm clause). In addition, the Bankruptcy Code itself has its own fraudulent conveyance statute (Section 548), under which recovery is limited by Section 550 to one year after the transfer.

In either case, fraudulent transfers may be divided into those transfers made with deliberate intent to frustrate creditors in their collection activities, on one hand, and those transfers in which the debtors received less than fair consideration, on the other hand.

The intentional transfer case might be exemplified by the transfer of the debtor's flock of sheep to his brother-in-law, who then employs the debtor as a shepherd on the eve of judicial seizure of the flock to satisfy a debt. This fact pattern caused the now infamous Court of Star Chamber to recognize "badges of fraud" (characteristics of fraudulent conveyances) in *Twyne's Case,* 3 Co. Rep. 80b, 76 Eng. Rep. 809 (Star Chamber 1601), which are still relevant today. The debtor who would rather give his pickup truck to his brother than let the sheriff seize it for creditors might be a modern day analogue. These cases seem to become more common when divorce proceedings complicate insolvency cases.

The "less than fair market value" type of transfer occurs more often in business cases. Some examples include the struggling debtor who sells property (sometimes including an entire division of the business or the entire business) for fire sale prices to satisfy immediate obligations. This fact pattern is sometimes complicated by personal guarantees, which may encourage the guarantor officers to "dump" property at less than fair value to ensure that guarantied obligations are satisfied.

Much more complicated are the leveraged buyout transactions wherein the assets of an operating business are pledged to secure payment of promissory notes financing the purchase of the business entity by new owners. This type of transaction is subject to avoidance because the (non-debtor) owners of the business entity benefit from the lien placed on the assets, but the business itself does not benefit. The granting of a lien to secure a loan is a transfer of property of the debtor, and it is this type of transfer which is customarily avoided in such cases.

A related problem involves guaranties of the indebtedness of a parent company signed by subsidiaries. When such guaranties are accompanied by a pledge or security interest to secure the guaranty, that transaction may be subject to avoidance. The question then becomes what benefit the subsidiary received from the loan.

Fraudulent conveyance cases tend to be very fact-intensive and are commonly tied closely to valuation issues. For bankruptcy lawyers, it is customary to consider fraudulent conveyance concerns carefully during the transactional process, to avoid litigating the same issues later. To eliminate the specter of a fraudulent conveyance attack following a sale, it is sometimes necessary to buy after a bankruptcy filing, through a court-ordered sale process, rather than attempt to get a phenomenal "bargain" from a company in dire straits. These issues frequently implicate business judgment issues, as well as legal analysis.

Chapter 15: The Creditors Committee
[Section 1103]

In Chapter 11 cases, the usual format is for the debtor to function as a "debtor in possession," remaining in control of its property and operating its business under Sections 1107 and 1108. Initially, no trustee is appointed. But the Office of the U.S. Trustee performs a nominal supervisory role, presides over the meeting of creditors, and receives written monthly operating reports.

And while a trustee can be appointed for cause, such appointments are fairly rare. Instead of a trustee functioning as a counterweight to the reorganizing debtor, Chapter 11 provides for the creation of an Official Committee of Unsecured Creditors. In certain cases, courts may also appoint other official committees, usually including an Equity Holders Committee. In complex cases, it is possible for other similarly situated groups to obtain official committee status, particularly in cases involving mass tort victims such as asbestos claimants.

The 2005 Reform Act also allows small business creditors to join the committee if their claims are disproportionately large in relation to their own gross revenues. This may be permitted even if their claims are significantly smaller than the claims of the other committee creditors. [See Section 1102(a)(4).]

The benefits of official committee status are several. Perhaps most importantly, the official committees are entitled to have their legal counsel paid for by the bankruptcy estate. Also, courts tend to accord some deference to the opinion of official committees on plan formulation and confirmation issues. Courts are aware that these issues frequently affect those creditors represented by the committee much more than secured creditors, whose full recovery is usually assured by liens and security interests. Additionally, official committee status assures a mechanism for disseminating crucial case information to committee members and those they represent, through the efforts of paid counsel.

Because most committees operate in cases where there is no trustee appointed, the role of official committees also encompasses "keeping the debtor honest." This is done by reviewing the business and financial information reported by the debtor, particularly regarding operating results.

Committees are frequently better at spotting conflicts between the debtor and its management than the Office of the U.S. Trustee. Committee members, in many cases, are financial officers of companies in the same industry, or a closely related industry, to that of the debtor. They are usually familiar with the finances and customs of the industry. Their actual industry experience makes them more effective in ferreting out inflated operating results or misleading information in disclosure statements, particularly when evaluating financial projections and the feasibility of proposed plans.

In some cases, the inability of the debtor to work with the official committees has been offered as a justification for replacing debtor management with a trustee. In most cases, debtors try very hard to win and keep the support of the committee and its counsel. The endorsement of a committee for a debtor's plan of reorganization is frequently viewed as essential for an affirmative creditor vote.

Service on a creditor's committee is not compensated time. However, committee members are entitled to reasonable expenses, such as travel, long distance, and fax charges. In most cases, those who serve on committees do so because the claim of their company is a substantial claim and they want to protect that investment.

Chapter 16: Sales of Assets
[Section 363]

The "363 Sale" is another one of those terms that make up the jargon of bankruptcy law. In straight (liquidation) bankruptcy cases, trustees often sell estate assets to raise money to pay a dividend to creditors. In fact, the term "liquidation" is derived from the reduction of assets to cash.

Section 363 provides that a trustee may sell assets outside the ordinary course of business, after notice and a hearing. This section also applies to Chapter 11 debtors in possession, who have the rights, obligations, and duties of trustees.

Bankruptcy sales of assets are often desirable in Chapter 11 cases for a variety of reasons. It may be necessary to raise cash for distribution under a plan. Corporations may need to refocus on their core business by divesting non-core assets. Or it may be that the debtor can no longer operate profitably and must "reorganize" by liquidating itself.

Buyers of assets in bankruptcy cases traditionally get very clean title. The order approving the sale and transfer of assets generally releases the assets (and the buyer) from all liens, claims, and encumbrances. These liabilities are attached to the proceeds of sale and are sorted out by the creditors and the court *after* the buyer leaves the case with the assets. Buyers are also insulated from fraudulent conveyance attacks by the judicial imprimatur. For this reason, most sophisticated buyers prefer to buy after the bankruptcy petition has been filed, and not before.

Sales of Assets

Sales are subject to objection from creditors on the grounds of:

(1) inadequate notice;

(2) their desire for an auction format; or

(3) the belief that a better price is available from other buyers.

Sales are also subject to objection if the sale is of such a substantial portion of the assets that it constitutes a de facto plan of reorganization or renders other potential plans unachievable. Selling debtors are required to demonstrate that sales are beneficial to the debtor in the business judgment of the board of directors. Boards are also bound by common law to maximize asset value.

Realistic buyers must understand that all sales can be turned into auction venues in bankruptcy cases and must be prepared to assume this risk of doing business. Buyers (ironically) are not considered parties in interest in most bankruptcy cases (unless they happen to also be creditors) and have limited rights to be heard.

Even so, 363 Sales often produce good results for sellers and buyers. The threat of fraudulent conveyance attacks alone is enough in many cases to cause buyers to wait for a 363 Sale. A "great deal" prior to bankruptcy may be recast, in hindsight, as a transfer for less than fair equivalent value. Such sales can be unwound under fraudulent conveyance laws (see Chapter 14), but the 363 Sale cannot be unwound, even if the purchase price seems low.

Chapter 17: Reorganization Financing
[Sections 363 and 364]

Business debtors typically enter Chapter 11 with most of their assets encumbered by mortgages, liens, or security interests. It is common for secured creditors to have control of key assets such as bank accounts, accounts receivable, inventory, equipment, and general intangibles through the provisions of their loan and security agreements. Outside the scope of Chapter 11, secured creditors can divert all of the debtor's funds to themselves and effectively put the debtor out of business.

Chapter 11 envisions debtors in possession continuing to use these assets to maintain operations and reorganize their finances. The theory is that the business should be able to operate at least long enough to be sold as a going concern. But the ideal situation would be for the company to operate its way out of debt with some help in the way of restructuring the balance sheet. For this reason, the code authorizes the use of "cash collateral."

Cash collateral means cash, cash equivalents, and proceeds of goods in which creditors have security interests. Instead of giving these assets to creditors to satisfy their debts, the Bankruptcy Code permits debtors to use the assets, provided that the interests of the creditors are adequately protected. Adequate protection means essentially that the creditor's chance of receiving full payment is not diminishing. To the extent the creditor's position gets worse, the debtor will be required to make up the difference through cash payments, additional liens, additional collateral, or some other mechanism approved by the court.

Reorganization Financing

Some debtors, especially large corporate entities, need new financing during the Chapter 11 case. This is commonly called DIP financing, because the loans are made to the *debtor in possession*. DIP financing must be approved by the court on notice to all parties. The most difficult part of this is finding a lender with an appetite for lending money to bankrupt entities. Several large banks, as well as a host of specialized hedge funds, have departments set up for DIP lending.

DIP lenders generally take advantage of the superpriority provisions of Code Section 364, which allow their liens to prime all existing liens in place. Doing so requires proof of adequate protection of liens. It has become common for DIP lenders to "take out" existing liens by paying off these secured debts. This action allows the DIP lender to avoid the adequate protection issues. In addition, it allows the lenders to make even more money by earning interest on all of the outstanding secured debt.

DIP financing involves, at least in theory, a higher degree of risk than standard lending. Consequently, most DIP packages include fees and high interest rates, which makes this financing very profitable for the specialized players who provide it.

As more commercial lenders have become aware of the advantages of DIP lending, the market for such financing has broadened. It is no longer uncommon for the smaller lender or the smaller debtor to present DIP lending arrangements for court approval.

Chapter 18: Leases and Contracts
[Section 365]

When a person or company files a bankruptcy case, they may be a party to one or many contracts or leases. In the case of an individual (natural person) debtor, these may be simple and run of the mill. For example, many people lease residential real estate such as apartments or houses. Also, many individuals are members of health clubs under ongoing contracts.

When a business files for bankruptcy, the contracts may be numerous and complicated, and they may either be valuable assets or economic millstones hung around the debtor's neck. Examples include:

- contracts to produce or sell goods;
- contracts to provide services or license technology;
- commercial leases ranging from tiny shops to entire shopping centers, office buildings, manufacturing facilities; or
- specialized real estate leases, such as airport departure and arrival gates.

The Bankruptcy Code deals with all of these legal relationships in Section 365.

Section 365 is now one of the longest and most complex sections in the entire Bankruptcy Code. Understanding its provisions requires, in addition to a grasp of its massive number of details, an understanding of the basic principles.

The fundamental rule is that trustees (or, in reorganization cases, the reorganizing debtors) may elect whether to assume (keep) the contract or lease or reject it. This rule is brilliant in its flexibility, and absolutely revolutionary in its departure from, and ultimate reaffirmation of, the principles of contract law. The rule is based upon the financial and business reality that there must be a means of escape from disadvantageous contractual obligations if bankruptcy relief is to be effective. The Faustian bargain is indispensable for morality plays and other fine art, but an economic system built on risk and reward would be stifled if a bad contract meant eternal poverty.

On the other hand, some contracts are tremendously valuable to the estate or the reorganizing debtor. By preventing the non-debtor party from canceling contracts because of bankruptcy, the code encourages use of these assets in reorganizations. This allows trustees and debtors in possession to benefit from assignment (sale) of the debtor's rights.

Section 365 is now a compendium of special rules for airline debtors, parties to shopping center leases, and licensors and licensees of technology, among others. Moreover, it contains some timing provisions for lease assumption or rejection that result in automatic rejection if certain actions are not taken within prescribed time periods after the case is filed. Put simply, this is no place for novices to roam alone—an experienced lawyer is a requirement.

The code ultimately reaffirms the basic principles of contract law by treating rejection of a lease or contract as a breach. However, the breach is treated as a pre-petition claim. This means that the debt created by the breach is subject to complete or partial discharge, even though the rejection occurs after the case is filed. The code also includes provisions to ensure that breach of contract claims do not unfairly dominate the distribution of assets to creditors. An entirely different section (Section 502) sharply limits the claims of lessors and terminated employees under employment contracts.

If a reorganizing debtor or trustee elects to assume a contract or lease, the whole contract or lease must be assumed. There is no ability for the entity to assume only the benefits and not the detriments of the deal. Assumption of the contract or lease requires cure of economic defaults on the part of the debtor and adequate assurance of future performance. The debtor or trustee, moreover, must assume the contract or lease to assign (sell) it, meaning that the defaults must be cured. However, a special provision in Section 365 relieves the estate from liability for the breaches of the assignee, and in this respect, the code assignment provisions depart again from non-code contract law.

Creditors, lessors, licensors, and other parties to ongoing contracts and leases with debtors have found Section 365 ripe for litigation. Some of that litigation has resulted in the many amendments of the statute that now render it very situation-specific. The variety of possible contractual arrangements probably means that no statute could anticipate them all. If a contract or lease is at issue in a bankruptcy case, victory for the trustee or debtor is by no means a foregone conclusion. Attorneys are often able to settle or win these disputes for the non-debtor party.

Chapter 19: Fees and Fee Applications
[Sections 327, 328, 329, and 330]

The hiring and compensation of lawyers for debtors, trustees, and committees is closely regulated by the Bankruptcy Code. The same is true of investment bankers and their attorneys, accountants for the debtor, committee, trustee, and various other professionals. These professionals are compensated by the estate. The statutory scheme is intended to ensure that money is not spent indiscriminately.

It is often repeated that the rules permitting professionals to be paid ahead of creditors justify close scrutiny. These rules work in two basic ways. First, the code requires that all professionals be "disinterested," meaning that they have no interest adverse to the debtor or creditors, and they represent no interest adverse to the debtor or creditors. The professional (lawyer, accountant, crises manager, etc.) must file an application to be appointed to perform services for the debtor, committee, or trustee. The application must be accompanied by a statement that the professional holds or represents no adverse interest. Additionally, there must be a comprehensive disclosure of any connections between the professional and his firm, and the debtor or creditors.

Once the professional is hired by order of the court, he or she must maintain very detailed records of time and charges expended. These records are subject to all sorts of rules and regulations, including:

- time must be kept in six minute increments;
- descriptions of the time spent must be accounted for, to the minute;

- records of phone calls must include name(s) of parties and subject matter discussed;
- descriptions of written work, with an itemized list of time spent on research and writing; and
- other similar rules.

Prior to being paid, the professional must submit a written fee application to the court. The Office of the U.S. Trustee is entitled to object to the fees if the description is incomplete, if the fees seem excessive, or if the services were not actual or necessary.

Fee applications normally must be submitted in four-month intervals. The fee application itself is a detailed piece of legal work, and the time spent on it is compensable. Parties in interest other than the U.S. Trustee are also entitled to object.

In practice, the issues which cause the most difficulty usually involve disclosure. Casebooks are replete with distinguished firms who encounter motions to disqualify them from the case and require disgorgement of fees, based on asserted failure to disclose potential conflicts. The cases range from documented conflicts of interest to breaches of disclosure technicalities.

In practical terms, the process of hiring professionals now requires a very detailed investigation of all potential creditors, including the names of their parents and affiliates. This is to ensure that professionals are not representing the potential creditors in some capacity. Representation of parties adverse to the creditors in lawsuits must be disclosed. And, with many law firms and professionals now working in cities across the country and throughout the world, the conflicts process can be particularly difficult to manage. This is especially true if the debtor's stock is publicly traded.

All of these details produce a somewhat game-oriented atmosphere, in which even diligent inquiries sometimes fail to reveal potential conflicts. Adverse parties often conduct their own investigation once the case is in full swing to attempt to disqualify lawyers or other professionals who present obstacles to the adverse parties' desires. In this atmosphere, debtors must allow extra time for the retention process to work. Seemingly insignificant connections to other parties may prevent the counsel of their choice from being eligible to represent them, or preclude the hiring of otherwise qualified accountants, investment bankers, or other professionals.

Chapter 20: Plans of Reorganization
[Section 1129]

The plan of reorganization is the centerpiece of Chapter 11. It groups the creditors into classes of similarly situated claims and proposes "treatment" of their claims. In essence, this means some payment or distribution of part or all of what they are owed, usually over time, but sometimes in a lump sum. The unpaid portion, if any, is discharged. The plan does not become effective unless the court enters an order confirming it.

Section 1129 provides a recipe for confirmation by the court. One of the ingredients is that each class of creditors (subject to a couple of important exceptions) accepts the plan. The process of acceptance is accomplished by a vote of each class of creditors, evidenced by a ballot sent to each creditor and returned to the debtor. Acceptance is measured by classes. There are special provisions in Section 1129 which may allow a court to "cram down" a plan of reorganization over the rejection vote of a non-accepting class.

Chapter 11 plans must include a strategy by which all creditors would be paid at least as much as they would receive if the case were converted to Chapter 7. This rule is known as the "best interests of creditors" test. It protects dissenting creditors even if all other creditors have voted to accept the plan.

The formulation of a Chapter 11 plan generally involves obtaining the consent of major creditors in advance or during the drafting process. Debtors get (with certain exceptions for single asset real estate cases) a period of 120 days to propose a plan, with the exclusive right to file it. After the expiration of the exclusivity period, creditors become eligible to file competing plans. The exclusivity period may be extended by the court for cause, but the Bankruptcy Reform Act of 2005 puts an absolute limit on the period of exclusivity at 18 months from the filing date.

It has become fashionable in recent years to obtain consent to plans by paying nearly all creditors 100% of their claims. In publicly held companies, this is frequently accomplished by wiping out the equity classes and issuing new stock to the funders of the plan. This treatment comports with the notion that creditors occupy a higher place in the corporate food chain than stockholders. But the de facto sale of the enterprise to a new group of equity owners usually means that the problems in the debtor's business are fixed by the new owners after the case is over.

The protections provided by Chapter 11 were intended to be used as a corporate hospital to fix the problems within the case. The current trend is to use Chapter 11 only as a corporate emergency room, where the patient is stabilized just enough to permit transfer to another department.

In this environment, it is productive for debtors to enter Chapter 11 protection with the plan as close to complete as possible. Doing so helps the debtor to remain in control of the case and minimizes potentially ruinous professional fees.

In some cases, not only the conceptualization, but also the drafting of the plan and the solicitation of acceptance can be accomplished prior to filing the case. The resulting plan is known as a "prepackaged plan" or a "prepack," and it is usually filed with the requisite acceptance, together with the petition. Prepacks are fairly rare.

In the more standard cases, the plan is filed after the petition, together with a Chapter 11 disclosure statement. The disclosure statement is a major document. It must provide "adequate information" to allow creditors to make an informed judgment as to how to vote on the plan. In practice, these documents often focus on financial projections, pro-forma balance sheets, and a liquidation analysis. The liquidation analysis is designed to demonstrate that the plan provides at least what creditors would receive in liquidation, thereby satisfying the "best interests of creditors" test.

Chapter 11 plans and disclosure statements are the heart of the business reorganization practice. They are the written embodiment of the business deals which allow the actual restructuring of balance sheets and permit productive businesses to continue to exist after insolvency threatens them.

Because of the critical importance of reaching a business solution to business-oriented problems, the focus in reorganization should always stay on these issues and not on the mechanical elements of the case and its many filings and procedures. Successful Chapter 11 debtors are able to focus on the problems which created the need for reorganization, embody solutions to those problems in a plan, and obtain consent of creditors to plan confirmation. Achieving these goals quickly usually means that most of the work is done before the case is filed. Prepetition planning is essential to the successful Chapter 11 case.

Chapter 21: Adversary Proceedings
(Part VII, Federal Rules of Bankruptcy Procedure)

The great majority of the bankruptcy practice is not adversarial in the same way that a case pending in the state or federal court system usually is. Bankruptcy cases usually do not involve trials and most individual debtors never see the bankruptcy judge who issues the discharge order in their case.

Adversary proceedings are exceptions to this general rule. They function as miniature lawsuits within bankruptcy cases. Adversary proceedings involve complaints, answers, pretrial conferences, discovery, witnesses, evidence, and trials in the bankruptcy court. Federal Rules of Bankruptcy Procedure (FRBP) adopt most of the Federal Rules of Civil Procedure, sometimes with a modification or two.

A good deal of these cases are fought over:

(1) avoidance actions, such as preferences or fraudulent conveyances;

(2) attempts by the trustee or debtor in possession to recover money or other property of the estate;

(3) attempts by creditors to deny the discharge or to limit the effect of the discharge as it pertains to a particular debt; or

(4) fights over revocation of confirmation of reorganization plans.

Lawyers who are not bankruptcy specialists frequently try adversary proceedings as these cases are very similar to other types of "straight" litigation. The Federal Rules of

Evidence apply, and the (fairly infrequent) changes to the Federal Rules of Civil Procedure included in Part VII of the FRBP are easy to spot, because the numbering systems are similar. There is a complete list of subjects of adversary proceedings in FRBP 7001.

Like cases pending in other courts, adversary proceedings are subject to settlement. Settlement is generally accomplished with a 9019 Motion. (See Chapter 22.) For the consumer debtor, the availability of the discharge is the issue most often litigated. The provisions of the bankruptcy code discourage some of this litigation by providing that the unsuccessful creditor must, under certain circumstances, pay the debtor's legal fees.

In business cases, the avoidance of preference claims is the issue litigated most often in adversary proceedings. Such claims are often assigned to the creditor's committee under the plan. This produces the somewhat odd result that unsecured creditors sue other unsecured creditors who received payment prior to the filing of the bankruptcy case. Such cases are nearly always settled instead of tried.

Chapter 22: Compromises of Claims
(Bankruptcy Rule 9019)

In bankruptcy cases, there is often some litigation or contested issue between the debtor and an adverse party. Whenever parties can agree, compromise is favored. Motions to settle contested matters or adversary proceedings are often referred to as "9019 Motions," in a shorthand reference to the rule.

The parties can compromise or settle however they choose, on the condition that one requirement is met—they must provide notice to all parties in interest in the bankruptcy case or their representatives on official committees. Notice of the agreement between the parties must be provided to all creditors, the trustee, the debtor, committees, and any other entity involved or interested in the bankruptcy proceedings, prior to any settlement. Notice must be provided by mail or by the best means practical under the circumstances, but no less than twenty days before the court holds its hearing on the proposed compromise.

The Rule 9019 Notice requirement is intended to keep all interested parties informed. Notice allows all interested parties to object to a proposed compromise. However, compromises are rarely objected to. The Rule 9019 Notice requirement also allows interested parties to monitor what is going on in the proceedings and the dealings between the debtor and other adverse parties.

Debtors may enter into numerous settlements throughout the course of bankruptcy proceedings. While settlement is favored, the notice requirement provides protection to all of the non-settling parties. A settlement will ultimately affect the amount of debtor funds available for distribution to interested parties and creditors. Sophisticated creditors may want to stay apprised of settlements to keep track of the debtor's remaining funds and payouts made to other creditors.

Should a debtor and adverse party enter into a settlement agreement without following the Rule 9019 Notice requirements, they run the risk that the agreement will be deemed unenforceable. However, if Rule 9019 Notice requirements are satisfied, no objections are filed, and the court approves the settlement, then the settlement order is final and enforceable.

Chapter 23: Involuntary Bankruptcy Cases
[Section 303]

Originally, all bankruptcy cases were involuntary and were intended as remedies of aggrieved creditors against insolvent debtors. We tend to consider modern bankruptcy in terms of relief for the debtor and, usually, in terms of imposing a debtor-oriented remedy in the form of the discharge of debt upon creditors. In fact, involuntary bankruptcy, filed by creditors against a non-paying debtor, remains a part of the current U.S. bankruptcy system although it is infrequently used.

This type of proceeding has its roots in Renaissance Italy, where traders sold goods from a bench in the town square. When a trader could not pay his debts as they came due, creditors would sometimes break his sales bench, effectively putting him out of business. The Italian phrase for broken bench, "banca rotta," is the antecedent for the term "bankrupt."

Modern involuntary cases, with some exceptions for very small cases, require the signatures of three petitioning creditors. Their aggregate claims must total more than $12,300, indexed to the cost of living. Also, the petitioning creditors must be able to prove that the debtor is generally not paying debts as they come due. If these conditions are met, the court will order relief, meaning that the debtor will be the subject of a bankruptcy case whether the debtor likes it or not.

The Bankruptcy Code provides that the subject of an involuntary petition can either acquiesce in the filing or controvert it. If the debtor elects to fight the case, the party can do so by filing an Answer to the petition, which requires the court to immediately conduct a trial.

Trials generally focus on the issues of whether the debts are the subject of a good faith dispute (which disqualifies the holder from petitioning creditor status) or whether the debtor does, in fact, generally pay its debts as they become due. Balance sheet insolvency (whether debts exceed assets on the books) is not an element of the equation.

An excellent and short primer may be found in the case of *In re The President of the United States,* 88 B.R. 1 (Bankr. D.C. 1985) in which a disgruntled veteran attempted to file an involuntary petition against Ronald Reagan in his official capacity as President. The veteran sought military back pay from 1943, alleged to total over $39 million with interest. The court ordered the clerk to reject the petition, because the government could not be a debtor under the express terms of the Bankruptcy Code. It also ordered rejection because sovereign immunity was not waived and because the petition was filed by only one creditor, not three. However, the court's analysis makes clear that it is only the rarest of petitions that justify rejection outright and the case considers many fundamental elements of involuntary bankruptcy.

While not invoked in the presidential case, the Bankruptcy Code includes certain penalties for filers who do not file in good faith. In some cases, those penalties extend to consequential damages and attorneys' fees.

It is common practice not to proceed with involuntary cases unless there is a compelling reason to do so. Often, the case is filed to unwind transfers which may be fraudulent conveyances or preferences, including judicial liens, mechanics or materialmen's liens, mortgages, or security interests. The unique opportunities to reverse these transactions in bankruptcy court may justify the risk, expense, and inconvenience of filing such cases.

Chapter 24: Bankruptcy Reform Act of 2005

On April 20, 2005, President Bush signed the Bankruptcy Abuse Prevention and Consumer Protection Act of 2005 (the "Reform Act") into law. The controversial law effects sweeping changes to the bankruptcy system. Unfortunately, the provisions of this amendment to the Bankruptcy Code were drafted by lobbyists for the credit card issuers and bankers. The legislation was pushed through Congress in an atmosphere of partisan politics and extreme catering to the financial industry. The fundamental assertion of creditors, that the American bankruptcy system had become too easy for debtors to manipulate, was never supported by real facts or figures. In fact, several distinguished authors have produced studies based on actual case histories which disprove the theory that abuse was often committed by debtors. Nevertheless, the new provisions have been enacted. Only case law construing them will resolve the many ambiguities in this fundamentally flawed legislation.

Consumer provisions: It will be harder for middle-income consumers to erase debts through the comprehensive discharge provided in Chapter 7. The new law creates a "means test," which is a complicated formula that compares the debtor's income to his or her expenses, and to state median incomes. If the analysis shows money available to service debt, the consumer will be taken out of Chapter 7, which does not require repayment of any debt, and put into Chapter 13, which requires payroll deductions in favor of a special trustee who pays creditors on a pro-rata basis. [See Chapter 2 and Section 707(b).]

Consumers will also have to attend mandatory credit counseling as a prerequisite to receiving a discharge in Chapter 7. [See Sections 727(a)(11); 521(b); and 109(h).]

Creditors should pay attention to offers for compromises of debts made through consumer credit agencies. If a creditor "unreasonably refuses" a compromise concerning unsecured consumer credit made more than sixty days before filing, the creditor might have its claim reduced in the bankruptcy case. [See Section 502(k).]

The Reform Act also impacts non-dischargeable debts. This will leave more debt in place even after the discharge. For example, domestic support obligations, certain educational loans (beyond just federal loans), loan repayments to retirement plans, and certain condominium and homeowner fees will be non-dischargeable under the new law. Consumer debts for "luxury goods" incurred within 90 days of filing, and debts for "cash advances" taken within 70 days of filing will be non-dischargeable. Similar debts were non-dischargeable before, but the act makes it easier to call something a "luxury good," reduces the threshold amount of an offending cash advance, and increases the time period for scrutiny of such transactions. [See Section 523(a).]

Under the Reform Act, the consumer debtor must wait eight years (previously six) after receiving a discharge in one case before receiving another discharge in a new case.

Exemption for retirement savings
[Sections 522(b)(3)(C), (b)(4), (d)(12), (n)]: All savings in accounts that are tax-exempt under certain sections of the Internal Revenue Code can be exempted from the estate up

to an aggregate of $1 million and the cap can be increased if justice requires. This change is in accord with recent Supreme Court case law. It encourages retirement savings by protecting these accounts.

State law exemptions [Sections 522(b)(3)(A) and 502(o)(p)(q)]: The Reform Act imposes a longer residency requirement (from 180 to 730 days) for debtors to elect to utilize a state's exemption scheme. This will discourage debtors from making a pre-bankruptcy move to a different state to obtain more favorable exemptions. The act imposes additional limits on the amounts that can be claimed under a state law homestead exemption, for property acquired within 40 months of filing, and if the debtor committed certain wrongful acts. These changes are consistent with the overall thrust of the act—tightening up on Chapter 7 debtors and making more money available to creditors.

Reaffirmation agreements [Section 524(k)]: The act contains enhanced requirements for approval of reaffirmation agreements where the debtor is not represented by counsel. The debtor must receive a long list of disclosures before signing. This portion of the act was designed to address perceived abuses in connection with reaffirmation agreements. All creditors should review the disclosure requirements prior to entering into any reaffirmation agreements.

Landlords can evict debtors [Section 362(b)(22), (l)]: Under the Reform Act, residential landlords can bypass the automatic stay in certain circumstances and proceed to enforce pre-petition eviction judgments 30 days after the petition is filed. However, the debtor has options to cure in the first 30 days. This change will be a welcome one for residential landlords.

Changes to Truth-In-Lending Act (TILA): The act creates enhanced TILA disclosure requirements related to the following subjects:

- minimum payments in an open-end credit plan;
- tax deductions where credit is secured by a consumer's dwelling;
- "teaser" rates;
- internet-based open-end credit solicitations; and
- late payments and penalties.

Further, lenders can no longer terminate a credit account because the consumer has not incurred finance charges.

More power for PMSI holders [Section 521(a)(b)]: In consumer cases, purchase money security interest (PMSI) holders get some help. As to personal property secured by a PMSI, the debtor must reaffirm, redeem or surrender the property within 45 days of the first meeting of creditors. If not, then after 45 days the property is no longer property of the estate, the automatic stay no longer applies to it, and the creditor can take action permitted by law (i.e., is free to repossess).

Debtors counsel certification [Section 707(b)(4), (C)]: Lawyers who sign the petition are certifying that they have performed a reasonable investigation of the circumstances giving rise to the petition and that it is warranted. Counsel is effectively certifying that the debtor's schedules are correct.

Business provisions—prepackaged bankruptcies [Section 341(e)]: The Reform Act allows the court to dispense with the Section 341 Meeting of creditors if the debtor has filed a prepackaged plan. The act also affects a debtor's ability to solicit votes. Under the Reform Act, a debtor that lawfully solicited votes from a creditor for a prepackaged plan before filing can make other lawful solicitations of the same creditor while the case is pending (and apparently regardless of whether a disclosure statement has been approved).

Debtors' ability to reject commercial leases [Section 365(d)(4)]: The act will require debtors to accept or reject commercial leases within 120 days of filing. Debtors can only get one non-consensual extension of 90 days. After that, the landlord must consent to any further extensions. This will prevent endless extensions of the deadline, giving commercial lessors new leverage in Chapter 11 cases.

However, the Reform Act does take something away from commercial lessors. Administrative (higher priority) damage claims arising from rejection of commercial leases are capped at two years' worth of rent after rejection or turnover. Further, the damages will now be reduced by amounts recovered by the lessor or those amounts which the lessor will recover from another source. Any damages in excess of these caps will be treated as general unsecured claims.

Investment bankers and their attorneys can be employed as professionals in a bankruptcy case [Section 101(14)]: Investment bankers and their professionals who were employed by the debtor prior to the bankruptcy case are no longer automatically disqualified as advisors under the Reform Act. This change should make major Chapter 11 cases cheaper and more efficient by reducing the learning curve for new professionals, thus allowing the debtor to work with those professionals most knowledgeable about its financial situation.

Limits on exclusivity [Section 1121(c), (d)]: The debtor has a period of time when it has the exclusive right to file a reorganization plan. When that period of exclusivity passes, others may file competing plans. Under the Reform Act, the period of exclusivity is 120 days. It can be extended, but the act places an absolute limit on the period of exclusivity at 18 months from the filing date. Consistently, the 180-day window for getting a plan confirmed cannot be extended beyond 20 months from filing. These changes are in accord with Supreme Court holdings emphasizing the need for expeditious reorganization. They also reflect the need to minimize the very high professional fees guaranteed by lengthy cases.

Changes to makeup and functioning of creditor's committee [Section 1102(a)(4), (b)(3)]: The unsecured creditors committee is a major player in Chapter 11 cases. The Reform Act will allow parties in interest to seek a change in the makeup of the committee to ensure it adequately protects creditors' interests. The act provides that a small business creditor can be added to the committee, even if the creditor has a smaller claim, if the claim is disproportionately large in relation to its gross revenues. The creditors committee also has enhanced reporting requirements to its constituents under the act.

Chapter 11 debtors must disclose financial details about companies they own or control: The act will require disclosure of information about the value, operations, and profitability of entities that the debtor owns or in which the debtor has a controlling or "substantial" interest.

Grounds for conversion or dismissal [Section 1112(b)]: The Reform Act tinkers with burdens of proof and adds more grounds for parties in interest to seek dismissal of a Chapter 11 case or conversion to Chapter 7. The "grounds" for obtaining such relief are expanded and are tied to the debtor in possession properly managing the estate. This will likely give more leverage to creditors as the case is pending.

Healthcare business bankruptcies [Sections 333, 351, and 704(a)(12)]: Healthcare entities must pay attention to several revisions that will affect administration of their case if they find themselves in bankruptcy court. First, the court must appoint a "patient care ombudsman" within 30 days of filing. The ombudsman will monitor patient care and periodically report on quality of care. If the ombudsman determines that patient care is declining, he or she must file a motion or report with the court. If a healthcare debtor has insufficient funds to store records, the act provides for notice and eventual destruction of records. Further, in a healthcare bankruptcy, the trustee must use best efforts to transfer patients if the debtor is closing down.

Employee wage and benefit claims [Section 507(a)(4)]: Employee wage and benefit claims are already entitled to priority, but the amounts are increased to $10,000 per employee. The period for accrual of priority wage claims has been increased to 180 days before the filing. This may create a need for more cash to get through a Chapter 11 because more money will be needed to pay these claims ahead of other creditors.

Unwinding modification to retiree benefits [Section 1114(l)]: If the debtor modified retiree benefits within 180 days before filing and the debtor was insolvent at the time of modification, the court shall (upon motion, notice, and a hearing of a party in interest) reinstate the benefits and unwind the modification. The court has discretion to deny reinstatement if equity favors the modification.

Important limitations on KERPS [Section 503(c)]: Many Chapter 11 debtors get permission to pay retention bonuses to key employees as part of Key Employee Retention Plans. Such plans will be subject to heightened scrutiny and outright numerical limits under the act.

Preference defendants get help [Section 547(c)(2), (c)(9) and 28 U.S.C. 1409(b)]: The Reform Act makes a small change to the ordinary course defense that will make the defense easier to maintain. Formerly, creditors had to prove that the transaction was ordinary, both subjectively (between the two parties at issue) *and* objectively (as to transactions in the industry). The Reform Act changes "and" to "or," therefore eliminating the need to prove, objectively and subjectively, that the transaction was in the ordinary course. Apparently, creditors can now choose either "subjective" or "objective" approaches to establish the defense. The Reform Act thus gives the ordinary course defense some additional punch. The act also provides that transfers of less than $5,000 cannot be avoided. This should curb the filing of mass-produced nuisance value preference complaints. Note that the floor in consumer cases is $600.

The Reform Act also requires that avoidance actions for business related claims be filed in the defendant's home jurisdiction if the claim is worth less than $10,000. However, if the defendant is an insider, the limit drops to $1,000. Note that the venue limitations should apply to all cases initiated by the trustee or debtor in possession, not just preference cases.

Warehousemen's liens [Section 546(i)]: The Reform Act provides that the trustee cannot avoid warehousemen's liens. Thus, the "strong-arm" powers of the trustee under Section 545 get decidedly weak when they approach a warehousemen's lien. The trustee is not permitted to set aside such liens for costs associated with storage, handling, and transportation of goods.

Utilities [Section 366(c)]: Utilities can stop service after 20 days unless the debtor provides assurance of payment. The Reform Act defines assurance of payment strictly— essentially requiring cash or an equivalent. The act "beefs up" already stringent requirements and allows utility companies to set off security deposits without notice or order of the court. This change, in conjunction with other changes, will create a heightened need for cash at the beginning of a Chapter 11.

Reclamation [Section 503(b)(9) and 546(c)]: Creditors that deliver goods to a debtor on credit have limited rights to reclaim those goods when the debtor becomes insolvent. Under the Uniform Commercial Code, a creditor must provide written notice of its intent to reclaim within 10 days of the debtor's receipt of the goods. The Reform Act helps creditors that might have reclamation rights in two important ways:

(1) creditors can reclaim goods sold on credit for the 45 days leading up to bankruptcy, so long as written notice was provided within 45 days of the debtor's receipt of the goods.; and

(2) creditors with a right of reclamation will have an automatic administrative (thus higher priority) claim for goods delivered within 20 days of the filing, as long as the goods were delivered in the ordinary course of business.

Even if the debtor consumed the goods or the goods are no longer in the debtor's possession, the creditor has an administrative claim for the value of the goods and can seek immediate payment for those goods delivered within the 20-day window. These important rights (enhanced time period for reclamation and administrative claims for goods shipped 20 days prior to bankruptcy) will give some trade creditors considerable leverage. This is another provision that will create a need for more cash at the beginning of a Chapter 11 case.

Even the government gets help [Sections 521(j), 1129(a)(9), 1141(d)(6)]: The Reform Act requires that a Chapter 11 plan must provide for regular cash payments for tax claims. All IRS tax liability must be eliminated within five years instead of the six years formerly allowed. The Reform Act further provides that corporate debtors are not discharged from tax liability which is the subject of a fraudulent return or which the corporation willfully attempted to avoid. Lastly, if the debtor does not file tax returns in a timely fashion, a taxing authority may move to dismiss or convert the bankruptcy case if the debtor does not cure within 90 days of such request.

Chapter 25: One Dozen Critical Pitfalls in Chapter 7 Consumer Cases

The 2005 amendments to the Bankruptcy Code have generated a lot of commentary, most of which is focused on means testing. However, many of the critical mistakes made in Chapter 7 cases involve fundamental failures to consider important elements of the case before it is filed. Once the filing is made, it is usually too late to change strategies, and the trustee may administer assets that the debtors thought they would keep.

Many of these pitfalls can be avoided by a careful examination of certain documents prior to filing. Of course, looking at these documents does not guarantee success, but it can help to avoid inadvertently providing the trustee with a surprise asset. Here are the "dirty dozen" most difficult pitfalls.

1. Failure to review recorded deeds to real estate

Debtors often do not understand the legal status of residential real estate. For example, when asked if they own real estate, many mortgagors will answer, "No," believing that the bank owns the house as a result of a mortgage. Understanding who does and does not own real estate is critical when planning a bankruptcy case, because the trustee steps into the shoes of the debtor. If the debtor owns real estate legally, the trustee will become entitled to take the real estate for liquidation purposes under certain circumstances.

For property ownership status, bankruptcy courts and trustees rely on recorded title. Recorded titles are those filed for record with local government agencies such as county recorders. Searching for title has become an easy task with the advent of computerized record keeping. Obtaining a copy with a recording stamp allows all parties to rely on the document.

Deeds to real estate may be held by a single debtor, jointly by married debtors, or by a debtor and other parties who are not filing bankruptcy cases. For example, siblings may be joint owners of a property inherited from parents, or a debtor may own a business property together with one or more partners.

Ownership affects exemption planning, among other things. In many states, married debtors filing jointly are each entitled to claim a real estate exemption if they are each owners. Knowing how real estate is titled is therefore essential to understanding how many exemptions are available. Believing wrongly that both spouses are entitled to an exemption could cause the trustee to object to exemptions wrongly claimed by non-owners and jeopardize the ownership status of the property.

In addition, property held by siblings or business partners together with the debtor can pose its own problems. Often, these are resolved by mortgages on the property consuming its value, making its taking unattractive to the trustee. Flying blind into this type of situation, however, is a needless risk.

Finally, some states have special protection for property held by co-owners who are spouses. Understanding the state law on this issue is important, because state and not federal law will determine the rights of the trustee to such property.

And, practitioners must view all of the state law determining ownership in conjunction with Bankruptcy Code Sections 363(f), (g), (h), (i), and (j). These sections provide special rules for trustee sales of property owned jointly by a debtor and other parties. In the case of a non-debtor spouse, sections 363(h), (i), and (j) impose certain conditions of sale on the trustee which may discourage such sales.

Most trustees demand to see copies of recorded deeds no later than the 341 Meeting. To properly schedule the property and plan for its continued ownership requires counsel to review and consider the implications of recorded deeds prior to filing. Relying on the debtor's understanding of ownership, which may be well-intended but wrong, can be a costly mistake.

2. Failure to review recorded mortgages

The great majority of real estate owned in the United States is subject to a mortgage or deed of trust. In fact, the primary reason trustees do not administer real estate as an estate asset is because the real estate is "under water," meaning mortgaged to its full value. Sales of property with no equity are of no benefit to the creditors and usually would be very harmful to the debtor. The first step in determining whether a trustee will sell real estate is to determine the fair market value and subtract the amount due under recorded mortgages.

In examining mortgages, counsel should insist on seeing documents obtained from the recorder's office. These documents must bear the recorder's official stamp. Counsel should review the property description, the names of the mortgagors, and the signature block, in order to ensure compliance with state law. If the mortgage is not properly witnessed or notarized, it may be subject to avoidance by the trustee.

Counsel should also check the date of the mortgage. If it is within the state fraudulent conveyance period of limitations, inquiry should be made into the use of the funds, especially in the case of a refinancing. And, if the mortgagee is not a financial institution, special scrutiny is warranted to determine whether the mortgage was recorded to hinder, delay, or defraud creditors.

Mortgages within the preference period (extended to one year if the mortgagee is an insider) are also deserving of special attention. Worst of all is the "phantom mortgage." This is a mortgage that the debtor is sure has been recorded (usually to secure a home equity line of credit), but the file does not show it. If the mortgage is not filed, the trustee is likely to take the real estate, even if the debtor was "sure" the mortgage was there!

3. Failure to examine tax returns

Tax returns may show income from stocks the debtor does not remember owning. The returns also may reveal discrepancies with the budget amounts claimed on Schedule I. They may also show a consistent pattern of substantial refunds. The trustee is going to examine at least two years of returns at the 341 Meeting. Counsel should be several steps ahead of the trustee.

The trustee is entitled to tax refunds owed to the debtor at the time the case is filed. Timing can be important but illusory in making the determination. The case filed on April

16 is an easy case to evaluate. The trustee will be entitled to the refund due for the previous year. However, if the case is filed on July 1st, and the previous year's refund has been received and spent, some trustees will still lay claim to one half of the refund due the debtors for the year of filing the bankruptcy case. Examining the return will allow counsel to see if a problem appears to be looming. Refunds are often substantial pieces of the debtor's financial planning and budget. Sometimes it is impossible to avoid paying the money to the trustee, but the debtors are entitled to know the risk of losing all or a portion of the refund.

4. Failure to plan the filing date to coincide with a low bank balance

Many debtors use a checking account as their primary means of paying bills. Debtors, like most holders of checking accounts, usually rely on their checkbook to account for their money. However, the trustee will look at a statement from the bank showing the amount on deposit as of the date of filing. This amount may be much higher than what the debtor's checkbook shows if some checks have not yet cleared.

This problem is often compounded by electronic deposit. If the case is filed heedlessly, the bank statement may show several thousand dollars in the account. In this instance, the trustee may force the debtors to turn over the non-exempt portion of the funds, even if the check had already been issued to creditors, such as mortgage holders.

Electronic terminals may provide the debtors with the ability to verify funds on deposit, either by personal computer or at an ATM. Most debtors generally have a sufficient grasp of available funds to minimize this problem. Counsel should try to help filers who are not as sophisticated to plan to file the case when their record balance is unnaturally high. With a bit of planning, most cases can be structured to stay at or near the exemption limit.

5. Failure to evaluate inheritance or insurance payments

It is very difficult to see bankruptcy problems compounded by the death of a relative, followed by the trustee seizing the inheritance or insurance. The Bankruptcy Code provides a special rule in Section 541(a)(5) for these assets, as well as for assets subject to divorce decrees (see following section). Specifically, these assets become property of the estate if the debtor becomes entitled to them before the filing of the petition or within 180 days thereafter. This rule is somewhat unique in deeming after-acquired assets part of the estate. Advance thought about these processes can avert some of the risk of an inheritance or insurance payment being lost.

Some circuits, notably the Sixth, now prohibit debtors from disclaiming an inheritance, using a fraudulent conveyance-based legal theory. Often, the only real planning that makes sense may involve a change in the will or beneficiary designation. These changes, obviously, must be instituted by the drafter of the will or owner of the policy on their own initiative. Moreover, such changes carry their own risks to the debtor. Inheritances or policy settlements not directed toward the debtor must be directed elsewhere. Should the testator or policy owner die while the changes are in effect, the debtor still will not receive the inheritance or policy proceeds. The changes could therefore require a subsequent change more than 180 days after the case is filed. This would put the debtor back into a position to collect the inheritance.

Obviously, there are a number of balancing points in this equation. Prebankruptcy planning is still part art and part science. As a result, the lawyer for the debtor usually should not be giving estate advice to the debtor's family members while the case is planned. However, if counsel advises the debtors about such points, the debtors can make their own decisions about discussions with family members.

6. Failure to review divorce decrees

Divorce decrees may award property to debtors over a substantial period of time. Some of this property may qualify as estate property under Bankruptcy Code Section 541(a)(5), even if it is received during the 180 days following the filing of the bankruptcy case. If the decree represents additional estate property, that property may require exemption planning. In addition, Bankruptcy Code Section 507(a)(1), amended under the 2005 Reform Act, now provides a new first priority payment for domestic support obligations. This provision may cause reluctance in trustees to administer property in certain cases. Trustees have historically viewed assets as worth administering only where general unsecured creditors are benefited. But as a result of this provision, all estate property may be distributed to a former spouse instead of general unsecured creditors.

Regardless of the ultimate implications of such decrees, the best time to review the decree is *prior* to the filing of the bankruptcy case, not after. Some former spouses can be quite vigorous in asserting their perceived rights. The assertion is often made in the form of a question regarding assets at a 341 Meeting. Counsel should be prepared for such questions, and the decree is an excellent place to start.

7. Failure to examine car titles

Trustees and bankruptcy courts evaluate ownership and lien issues pertaining to motor vehicles based on the certificate of title issued by the each state. In order to properly schedule motor vehicles as assets the attorney must look at the title to determine legal ownership. Evaluation of a trustee's claim to the car, or the planning of reaffirmations or surrender of the vehicle(s), requires an examination of the recorded lien of the title.

Debtors often do not understand ownership or lien issues. A debtor whose college student son drives one of the debtor's two cars at college in another state may regard the car as his son's property. The trustee, upon examination of the title, may take a different view. Also, creditors may fail to record liens on the title, especially (surprisingly enough) with new cars. If the lien does not appear on the car title, the trustee may avoid the secured claim and sell the car for the benefit of unsecured creditors.

With enough advance notice and planning, these problems can usually be corrected outside of the preference period. Debtors are usually not sufficiently familiar with the legal requirements to do this on their own. Counsel should therefore insist on seeing the titles early in the planning process.

8. Failure to review bank account statements

The trustee is going to insist on seeing bank statements for the filing date at the 341 Meeting. Counsel should ask to see the last statements in the debtor's possession at the first meeting with the clients, in order to see how the accounts are titled.

Joint accounts are entitled to twice the exemption available for accounts held in one name in most states, assuming that the married debtors file jointly. Also, accounts held in both names may be split in half for ownership purposes if only one spouse files. Asking for all statements may also force debtors to confront the status of "retirement accounts" (see section 9 of this chapter).

Finally, it is important to evaluate accounts held for children, elderly parents, or in other similar circumstances. Such accounts should be scheduled as property held for another person. This also applies to probate or trust accounts or similar assets. Failure to schedule these accounts may cause the trustee to suspect fraud.

9. Failure to examine "retirement accounts"

The 2005 Reform Act broadens the scope of exemptions available for retirement funds subject to favorable rulings from the IRS. (See Section 522 of the U.S. Bankruptcy Code.) However, some debtors hold unusual "retirement" accounts that may not qualify. Some debtors, in fact, consider their ordinary savings accounts as retirement accounts, based only on their intent to use the funds once they retire. The trustee and the court are not likely to recognize such informal designations. It is essential for counsel to see how the accounts are "plated" (named at the financial institutions) early in the process.

All 401(k) plans and IRAs should now be exempt at least up to an aggregate value of $1 million, and possibly more in some circumstances. These assets probably do not require the most scrutiny. State exemption laws (or the federal exemptions in states where they apply) must still be consulted where plans may not have received a favorable IRS determination letter.

10. Failure to schedule tort claims

A surprising number of debtors are plaintiffs in tort cases. Tort cases include car accident cases, negligence cases, wrongful termination cases, workplace harassment claims, assault, libel and slander, and other common types of lawsuits. These claims are assets when held by a debtor and must be scheduled and disclosed to the trustee and creditors.

When such claims are not scheduled, it creates an appearance of fraud which may be quite erroneous. Defendants, however, are adept at using the presumption that the debtor intended to discharge debts and retain the claim as a personal asset. This, of course, can jeopardize the tort case verdict or settlement.

Many states provide relatively generous exemptions for tort claim settlements, but such exemptions must be claimed by the debtor. Obviously, the exemption cannot be claimed if the attorney does not know about the case. Scheduling the asset applies to any claim occurring before the bankruptcy case, whether suit has been commenced or not. Attorneys must ensure that their clients understand the need to disclose such cases, on pain of possibly losing the benefit of discharge, as well as the court case, itself.

11. Failure to caution debtors to stop using credit cards

In the age of the credit economy, America's national savings rate is literally at zero percent of earnings. This statistic results, in part, from the fact that the engine of consumer spending which drives the U.S. economy is fueled by credit. Against this backdrop, it should be no surprise that many debtors live on cash advances, purchase gasoline, clothing, and even food with credit cards. Debtors sometimes use cash advances from one credit card to pay another.

When debtors use credit cards knowing that they will not pay the debt (because it is going to be discharged in bankruptcy) credit card issuers are afforded the opportunity to object to discharge on fraud grounds. This option has always been available. The 2005 Reform Act seeks to make it easier for the card issuer to use.

Section 523(a)(2)(C) presumes consumer debts owed to a single creditor aggregating more than $500 for "luxury goods or services" incurred on or within 90 days before the filing to be nondischargeable. Also, under Section 523(a)(2)(C), cash advances aggregating more than $750 within 70 days before filing are presumed nondischargeable. "Luxury goods or services" do not include goods or services reasonably necessary for the support or maintenance of the debtor or a dependant. Nevertheless, the best practice is to discontinue all card use once the decision to file has been made, to forestall the fraud argument. One exception to this rule might be for cards kept current or which are expected to be reaffirmed.

12. Failure to budget

Schedules I and J of the Bankruptcy Code constitute a rudimentary household budget. Schedule I tracks income, while Schedule J tracks expenses. Whether these forms (which are required with a filing) or a more simple format is used, the budgeting process is an important skill for debtors. Unfortunately, this skill is not taught in most public schools, and many debtors do not understand it.

In Section 727(a)(8), the 2005 Reform Act extended the prohibition on receiving a discharge in a second case until eight years after the discharge in a prior case. Previously, debtors were required to wait six years. In either case, no debtor wants "season tickets" to the bankruptcy court. Sadly, the filing of a petition may provide the debtor's only chance to discuss budgeting with a professional.

Bankruptcy is an escape hatch. Once it is used, it cannot be used again for at least eight years. Budgeting, in the post-petition period, may be more critical than ever before for the debtor. The great majority of people can and do live within a budget. Helping debtors to do so is possibly the most important benefit counsel can confer on an average consumer client.

Chapter 26: Ten Critical Questions to Answer Before Filing a Personal Bankruptcy Case

The decision to file a personal bankruptcy case is a complex blend of financial, legal, and emotional factors. Some people, even those who have eventually risen to the pinnacles of success and influence, were once unable to convince themselves that bankruptcy filing was an acceptable course of action. Others, such as Donald Trump and silver trader Nelson Bunker Hunt, have seen the wisdom in the utilization of these laws and have found a way to achieve their lofty goals after discharging otherwise insurmountable indebtedness.

After World War I, future United States President Harry S. Truman and his longtime friend Eddie Jacobson opened a haberdashery in Missouri. When the store failed, Jacobson discharged his debts in a personal bankruptcy. Truman, in contrast, worked for many years to repay the debts and was apparently successful in doing so.

The point of the Truman story is that for many prospective filers, the "shame" factor is too much to overcome. However, that argument, taken to its logical conclusion, produces very unhealthy and sometimes fatal results. Investors who were financially devastated by the stock market crash of 1929 occasionally killed themselves. Until quite recently, suicide was expected of top directors and executives of financially failed Japanese corporations.

Assuming that financial failure is not the result of fraud, the message may be to "just get over it." It is probably foolish for an individual to devote undue emotional stress to the consequences of an honest financial failure. One wonders how much good a person of Harry Truman's strength of character might have accomplished in lieu of sacrificing every waking moment to the repayment of debts of a failed business! Many creditors, such as credit-card issuers, have anticipated this reality and have reserves set aside to compensate for their losses due to the insolvency of some debtors. As a result, the self-inflicted emotional pain suffered by the debtor related to the filing may be entirely wasted.

The decision of whether or not to file a personal bankruptcy case is best evaluated by discussing the specifics with an experienced bankruptcy lawyer. The lawyer should be able to see the forest as well as the trees. The insight provided by an experienced insolvency attorney can add a valuable perspective to the potential filer's specific situation. Here are some key questions for counsel and client to explore before filing:

1. What caused the financial problem?

Bankruptcy is a way to rebalance the financial books and start fresh. However, the problem may recur quickly if it is not accurately diagnosed and corrected. Common causes of severe personal financial stress include:
- divorce
- illness
- loss of employment
- personal liability for business debt (guarantees)
- assisting family members with catastrophic problems
- failure to understand budgeting
- bad purchasing decisions
- overuse of credit

Too often, a number of these factors coalesce into a "perfect storm" of insolvency. For example, losing a job soon after buying a new car or an expensive house can leave a debtor with far too few financial reserves to pay debts until new employment is found. Losing a job also frequently results in loss of insurance benefits, especially health insurance. Divorce, too, can separate people from insurance and consume emergency savings.

Debtors need to have a clear understanding of the issues which forced them to file the bankruptcy case in order to avoid repeating the process of acquiring too much debt. This is critical, because the safety net of Chapter 7 will not be available for eight years after a discharge is issued. It is also important to understand the cause of the problems to ensure that bankruptcy will fix it. Personal dependencies such as chronic gambling, chronic spending, or even the simple failure to understand how to budget money require more than a bankruptcy filing to correct the underlying problem.

2. Are more problems on the horizon?

Uninsured illness (or even insured illness) can quickly create debts that would wipe out even the most carefully accumulated life savings. Filing a personal bankruptcy case while such an illness is progressing can be a costly mistake. It is generally better, if at all possible, to defer the filing until all of the expenses are on the books. Similarly, the chronic gambler or a person in the throes of other addictions may well need to file a bankruptcy case later rather than sooner to gain a lasting benefit.

3. Will a discharge of existing debt solve the problem?

This question is related to the previous two questions offered for consideration. If the cause of the debt is a failed business, an improvident purchasing decision (such as buying too expensive a house or car) or the sudden loss of a job, then it may be that the decision to file makes good sense. If, however, the cause is unwillingness to budget, lack of ambition, addiction, depression, or other chronic illness, it may make sense to try to cure the other problems first. Separating such ancillary considerations from the debtor's emotional responses may be one of counsel's most important contributions to the process.

4. Have the alternatives been explored?

Here are some commonly explored alternatives to filing a personal bankruptcy case:

- temporary second job
- refinancing a house
- seeking help from family members
- terminating help to family members
- making deals with creditors
- selling assets

There are a good many cases where none of these alternatives will work. For example, taking a second job will do no good if the amount earned will be consumed by child care. Refinancing a house is risky because it increases the chances of losing the house in foreclosure. Paradoxically, under certain circumstances, it may protect the residence from sale by a trustee. Seeking help from family members (in the form of temporary free lodging or loans) will do little good if catastrophic accident or illness costs are very large.

Terminating help to family members often comes too late to save the ship. Parents often consume their savings and then borrow money on credit card cash advances or home mortgages to help foundering children, especially adult offspring. Family loyalty is commendable, but the bankruptcy of only the younger generation may sometimes be preferable to the bankruptcy of both children and parents.

Making deals with creditors is sometimes feasible where business debts have been guaranteed by individuals. This type of situation usually works because there are a limited number of creditors and because they can see that no assets would be available to pay the debt. It usually does not work, however, when dealing with credit-card issuers or personal finance companies. Some debtors, after attempting to work with such creditors, find it easier to file bankruptcy instead of trying to make payments. It is inexplicable that credit-card issuers have long refused to take some but not all money due them outside the scope of bankruptcy.

Selling or refinancing assets is sometimes helpful. Most people, however, consume savings and saleable assets early in the process of being indebted. Because these alternatives are very fact sensitive, they should be explored with professional counsel. What works in some debt circumstances may not work at all in others.

5. Does the post-petition budget work?

Schedules I and J require projecting a rudimentary post-petition budget. Sometimes this budget emphasizes the need to earn more or spend less or both. Remarkably, some debtors are astonished at how many expenses must be included. Insurance, medical bills, real estate taxes, and income taxes are common "surprise" elements of budgeting. Going into a bankruptcy case without a workable post-petition budget is a self-defeating behavior. A lawyer can serve as a reality check in the budgeting process.

6. What assets are in jeopardy without a filing?

Social security income is exempt from garnishment by creditors. Leased housing and cars cannot be seized, either. And many states provide generous exemption laws applicable outside of bankruptcy. It is important to know what assets are in jeopardy in evaluating not only whether to file a bankruptcy case, but also when. Just as important, assets in particular danger, such as funds deposited with a creditor bank, may be placed in a safer place (legally speaking) if the danger is known. Once again, experienced counsel is a requirement in evaluating asset risks.

7. Should retirement assets be used to pay creditors?

The answer to this question is almost always a resounding "NO!" Retirement assets are protected by federal law so that they are available when income from employment ends. The laws protecting these assets (such as 401(k) plans, IRAs, and similar vehicles) are designed to prevent poverty and dependence in old age. As long as the money is left in the plan, creditors cannot touch it, even in bankruptcy. However, the same is not true if the funds are withdrawn. Instances in which all of the retirement assets are consumed in trying to avoid the inevitable bankruptcy filing are among the most heartbreaking cases in the law. To discourage use of these funds prior to retirement, withdrawals are often the subject of substantial additional tax penalties. Leave the retirement funds for retirement!

8. Is Chapter 7 available?

Prior to the 2005 Reform Act, Chapter 7 was always available to individuals. The Reform Act imposes a congressionally approved "means test" drafted by lobbyists for the financial industry. The goal of this test is to force middle- class debtors into Chapter 13. The means test is based on a radical view of the doctrine of substantial abuse of bankruptcy. This perceived (but unsubstantiated) view of bankruptcy abuse is the basis for the new rules, denying formerly eligible debtors the relief of the comprehensive Chapter 7 discharge.

The new bankruptcy forms include a rather complicated multipage schedule. The form has been written like a federal income tax return in which income and expenses are quantified according to statistical standards. The new form requires debtors to proceed in Chapter 13 instead of Chapter 7 if it is determined that 25 percent of unsecured claims could be paid to creditors over five years in Chapter 13. Alternatively, the court is required to dismiss the case. If the relief of Chapter 7 is available to the debtor, it is nearly always better for debtors than the constrictions of Chapter 13.

As this book goes to press, there is no case law on the means test. As the law develops, many of the ambiguities in the statute will be resolved by court decisions. Fitting personal cases into Chapter 7 by using the means test to the maximum legal benefit of debtors will be an important skill for personal bankruptcy lawyers working with the 2005 Reform Act.

9. What does a Chapter 13 plan require?

Chapter 13 uses the concept of a partial discharge, with the rest of the debt repaid to creditors by the debtor under the terms of a Chapter 13 Plan of Reorganization. Creation of a Chapter 13 plan requires some artistry to minimize the amount paid by the debtor. Chapter 13 trustees and practitioners take somewhat non-uniform approaches to the workings of the plans in various judicial districts in the United States. One consequence of the 2005 Reform Act may be more standardization of the Chapter 13 practice.

One key question is how much income must be paid to the trustee. Once these plans are implemented, they usually run for five years, so it is important not to overpay. Budgeting is extremely important in these cases. When consulting with an attorney, it is critical for the debtor to understand the workings of the Chapter 13 Plan and how much money it will take (via payroll deductions) to fund it.

10. Can I get back into the financial game?

Bankruptcy cases are temporary, not permanent. Even Chapter 13 ends after five years. Banks offer secured credit cards (which require a deposit and limit charges to the funds on hand) which provide a way to re-establish credit. At the time of this writing, there is an all-time record surplus of funds available over actual borrowing. As a result, the credit market will not permanently freeze out very many participants, even those who have discharged debt in a bankruptcy. Credit will again become available, albeit, gradually.

At one end of the extreme are tycoons such as Donald Trump, who have won and lost fortunes multiple times and who have sometimes sought refuge in bankruptcy. At the other end are those individuals who never seem to get a break. In the middle are the great majority of debtors, who address a marked low point in their financial life with a bankruptcy filing, and recover their financial stability thereafter. Many of these filers go on to great financial success, even though the personal filing appears on an individual's credit record for ten years.

Whatever may be the impediments to wealth and security, bankruptcy is not an insoluble problem. Like most hurdles in life, bankruptcy is survivable and temporary. If it can reasonably be avoided, it should be. If not, it should be taken seriously, but kept in perspective. For those who desire financial success, the opportunities will still be available after a bankruptcy filing.

Chapter 27: Ten Critical Questions to Answer Before Filing a Chapter 11 Business Reorganization Case

Chapter 11 business cases are often the last resort for financially troubled companies. These cases are designed to preserve existing businesses by eliminating crushing debt burdens. This goal is achieved, if it is achieved at all, by the court's order confirming a plan of reorganization. The confirmation order makes the terms of the plan of reorganization binding on all creditors and parties in interest.

The plan itself generally provides that some of the company's debts are paid, often over extended terms, while the remaining debts are discharged. Plan terms often include new equity, sales of assets, mergers, new ownership, new loans with terms favorable to the debtor, or other mechanisms to improve the balance sheet. Obtaining a court order confirming the plan, however, is a huge hurdle.

By some counts, only about 15 percent of Chapter 11 cases result in confirmed plans. The remaining cases end in conversion to Chapter 7 (liquidation) or dismissal (generally leaving the company to be dismantled by creditors). The odds are better for very large businesses and worse for smaller ones. Answering these ten critical questions and using the answers as discussion points between counsel and clients can help with the decision of whether to file.

Ten Critical Questions—Filing Chapter 11 Business Reorganization

1. What caused the financial problem?

Common causes include:
- lack of demand for goods or services,
- tax issues,
- bad contracts or leases,
- loss of key employees,
- overstaffing,
- bad management or bad planning,
- undercapitalization,
- loss of major customers,
- technological changes,
- foreign trade competition.

Sometimes, several of these causes intersect. Prospective Chapter 11 debtors should understand that Chapter 11 is partly about law, but mostly about business. It provides a short timeframe for fixing complex business problems. Trying to fix a troubled business in Chapter 11 without a concrete understanding of what the problems are is like trying to go on a long trip through hostile countryside without a map. Frankly, the only debtors who succeed are the ones who grasp the problems and know how to correct them.

2. What does the plan say?

All Chapter 11 cases proceed toward the goal of confirming a plan of reorganization. The plan classifies claims and provides a "treatment" for each class. Essentially, the treatment of each class means whether it is paid any money or property, how much, and when. A Chapter 11 plan usually discharges some portion of indebtedness and provides terms for the repayment of the rest. Creditors will each receive a ballot and will vote to accept or reject the plan.

The plan also provides for ownership of the stock of the reorganized entity and how much, if anything, the new or current owners pay for it. It is common to offer stock in partial or complete repayment of debt. In the process, the former stockowners are often completely wiped out. In cases where new stock is issued to former owners, they must give value (money, not "sweat equity") for the stock. Owners of shares in non-public corporations are often officers, directors or employees who rely on their stock ownership both to exert some control over the company and to build equity for retirement. Such individuals must made be aware prior to filing that they may lose their ownership interest in the company, or they may be required to pay money for new stock.

Reorganization Plans often incorporate:

- new financing;
- sales of some or all property;
- new owners;
- mergers;
- divestiture of non-core business assets; or
- other business or economic "fixes" for the problems that caused the need for the case.

When preparing a Chapter 11 case, it is important to know, almost from the first day of the planning process, what the plan will contain and how the business problems will be fixed. The inability to conceptualize the plan before filing, and to vet it within the company and its advisors, nearly guarantees failure.

3. Will the secured creditor support the reorganization process?

In some cases, the secured creditor (usually, a bank with a lien on all assets) can be persuaded to support the reorganization process. Support from the secured creditor can come in many forms. The creditor may approve of the debtor's continuing use of cash in which the secured creditor retains a lien. Or it may make new loans available to support operations or the payments called for in the plan. It may also rewrite the terms of promissory notes to extend payment or reduce interest.

In other cases, the relationship with the secured creditor is hostile or may become hostile quickly. Some of this depends on temperament of the parties, some on planning and approach, and some of it depends on the causes and proposed cures for the financial problems. In most cases, getting and keeping the support of the secured creditor is very important to the debtor. Consequently, counsel will usually try to craft a plan that treats the secured creditor somewhat favorably, while also providing favorable financing terms for the debtor upon plan confirmation.

Achieving both goals is not as difficult as it sounds. Sometimes, the secured creditor has "deal fatigue" and wants to be replaced by another lender. In other cases, the secured creditor is willing to lower the interest rate on the secured loan, or extend the terms, or make other concessions to the debtor. But this generally occurs only after the uncertainty of Chapter 11 is cured with a confirmed plan. Counsel for the debtor usually tries to understand the secured creditor's position early and works to negotiate plan terms that are beneficial to both the debtor and secured creditors.

The Bankruptcy Code supplies a number of negotiating points for the debtor and secured creditor including:

- use of liened cash (cash collateral) during the case;
- the extent to which the secured creditor will be paid on its notes during the case; and
- requests for the secured creditor to lend additional funds during the case (DIP financing).

In some cases, the interest rate or other terms of the notes are, themselves, among the problems the debtor most urgently needs to fix. This also provides room for negotiations between the parties. Negotiations in the most hostile cases may revolve around several issues. The secured creditor may negotiate to avoid being forced to accept the plan treatment by the court. This is sometimes referred to as "cram down." The secured creditor may negotiate the terms for replacing itself with another lender. Or there may be threatened litigation between the debtor and the secured creditor, which is resolved through negotiations in the plan context.

Understanding the dynamics between the debtor and secured creditor is critical for management and counsel. Sometimes, counsel and crisis managers can get secured creditors past lack of trust in current management and induce them to cooperate in the debtor's reorganization through a DIP (Debtor in Possession) financing facility. DIP financing can be very profitable for the bank while simultaneously improving the security and terms of the loan from the bank's perspective. These issues require close attention at the very beginning of the process.

4. Can the debtor afford the fees and costs?

Chapter 11 is nearly prohibitively expensive for most debtors. The filing fee alone for the case is $839. Then, the U.S. Trustee is entitled to a quarterly fee. This fee is based on disbursements through the Debtor in Possession account and is usually several thousand dollars. The debtor must pay for its own legal counsel, crisis managers, and accountants, as well as the fees earned by legal counsel, accountants, and other professionals hired by the official committees. These "professional fees" can be ruinous if not properly managed.

Properly "managing" fees, in the current environment, means keeping the case short in terms of total time spent from filing to plan confirmation. Short cases ensure among other things, that a large part of the work is done before committees are formed. Prior to filing the case, the debtor is paying only its own professionals and not committee professionals. When possible the plan and disclosure statement should be filed with the petition. Keeping the case short is the only way to minimize the number of professional hours billed, particularly by committee professionals. Fees in relatively small cases, even if run efficiently, are nearly always well in excess of $100,000.

Planning for these fees is the only way to manage them. Typically, secured creditors are asked to loan at least part of the funds to pay such fees as part of DIP financing or Chapter 11 exit facilities. Good counsel will rarely accept an engagement as debtor counsel without a substantial retainer, often in six figures. The expense incurred to complete a Chapter 11 case will often seem well worth it once the plan is confirmed and the company is out of jeopardy. But the expenses look enormous at the beginning. The fees are part of the process and must be anticipated and viewed as a cost of reorganization.

5. What are the potential personal tax liabilities for officers and directors?

Some corporations fail to remit federal withholding taxes or state sales taxes during periods of financial crisis. These taxes are known as "trust fund" taxes, because the money is collected from employees or customers and held "in trust" by the company until paid to the tax authority.

Failure to pay these taxes can result in personal liability to responsible parties. "Responsible parties" are officers or owners with authority to pay the taxes. The liability attaches when they decide to use the funds to pay non-tax creditors. This liability can be very hard to satisfy. It is not dischargeable in personal bankruptcy, not that personal bankruptcy is a desirable option, anyway!

For officers and owners, advice at the beginning of the process is in order. If a potential trust fund tax problem exists, it should be evaluated. Federal tax claims are accorded priority among unsecured claims by the Bankruptcy Code. This being the case, it may be possible to cure the problem by making one or more payments. Most importantly, no individual should be expected to incur such liability during the reorganization case. If the taxes can't be paid by the debtor during the bankruptcy case, it is a clear signal that reorganization should not be pursued.

6. Is the company worth saving?

Decisions surrounding a Chapter 11 filing usually have an emotional component. This is particularly true if the business is a community landmark or has been passed through generations of family ownership. The emotional issues can sometimes crowd out hard-nosed business decisions. This process can threaten the last chance to correct business problems in Chapter 11. Saving a failing business in Chapter 11 requires more than desire. It also takes insight into the root causes of the financial problems and workable business deals to solve them.

Foreign competition is now more of a threat to U.S. businesses than ever before. In a truly global marketplace, labor, fuel, and raw materials often cost a small fraction of U.S. standards when purchased overseas. Impending financial failure can sometimes be forestalled with technological innovations, willingness to take less profit, concessions from labor, or similar moves. More often, sale to a competitor or a merger with a stronger company may be the only way to avoid liquidation in Chapter 7.

For owners of some businesses, it may make more sense to close the company and work for someone else. Chapter 11 reorganization is incredibly stressful and success of the reorganization efforts is not a certainty. Chapter 11 cases run the gamut from lost causes to most likely to succeed. Consider an established company that is attempting to sell typewriters in the computer age as one extreme case. At the other end of the spectrum would be companies which are very workable with new cash infused by new or current equity owners. A proper evaluation of the benefits of filing the case should always include consideration of alternatives, including sale, liquidation, or closing the business without any type of bankruptcy filing.

7. Is any help available to managers?

Being the captain of a ship in the waters of Chapter 11 is a complicated task. It is, among other things, hard to know whether the ship is on course or headed for an unseen iceberg. The polar star, for navigational purposes, is whether the plan will fix the financial problems well enough that the company can survive. This depends, in large part, on whether a profitable core business exists within the company (see section 8, below).

Testing the assumption that the business can succeed with accountants, others in the company and industry, and especially counsel for the debtor, makes sense. In addition, there are a number of "workout" or "crisis management" firms whose professionals are available to help manage troubled companies. Such professionals are often expensive, with fees similar to legal fees. However, they are able to bring to the table valuable experience in managing financially troubled businesses, and in crafting and negotiating plans. Such managers can also provide a "reality check" in assessing the chances for success.

These crisis managers are often valuable sounding boards for existing officers and directors. Hiring such a firm, where it is economically feasible, may take the "heat" off of current management. This is especially true if the banks or other secured lenders have lost faith in management. Lenders may wonder if ineptitude at top levels is the "real" reason that Chapter 11 is in prospect. The involvement of these professionals can help to alleviate the lenders' fears. Hiring a crisis manager does not mean that current management is ousted. It is routine for crisis managers to serve only in a consulting role, leaving decision making to the company's owners or managers.

If a crisis manager is on hand to help test the feasibility of the plan, so much the better. If not, management should try to "measure twice and cut once" by scrutinizing the plan's provisions carefully in-house and also with the lawyers and accountants. The job is too important, too demanding, and too complex to rest on the shoulders of a single individual.

8. Does a profitable "core business" exist?

Some businesses function best on a small scale. Others need more volume to run profitably. Often, a business expands too quickly to be well managed. Sometimes it may simply expand to the wrong size and just gets "stuck" there.

In these cases, it is critical to perform the simple exercise of determining whether the company can be operated at a consistent and reliable profit at any size. For reorganization purposes, it is infinitely better to run a small company at a modest but consistent monthly profit than to run a much larger company at break-even or below. Often, this involves operating only the most profitable portions of the business and jettisoning the less profitable portions. Isolating the profitable parts of the business can entail a somewhat intricate analysis.

This analysis needs to be performed cold-bloodedly, without the intrusion of sentimentality. Right-sizing the business quickly may involve the pain of terminating some jobs. Failure to do so may result in the loss of the entire enterprise and hence, the loss of all of the jobs.

9. How will employees, customers, and competitors react to a Chapter 11 filing?

As difficult as Chapter 11 is from a technical point of view, communication and maintenance of relationships with important constituencies such as employees, customers and competitors can be equally challenging. Competitors often try to convince prospective customers that Chapter 11 means the end of the company. They do so to steal the business, of course. This needs to be anticipated and counteracted with communication. Long-term relationships with customers are usually built on trust and respect. Many customers have faced tough financial problems themselves. Customers are often surprisingly loyal in such circumstances if they are treated with honesty and respect.

Employees will have a different set of problems. They need to understand that Chapter 11 will not affect pay or vacation time or other benefits. Also, top employees may well be recruited by competitors, usually with the same "doomsday" predictions the competitors use with customers. Treating employees with honesty and respect, and taking every opportunity to communicate with them, is of critical importance. These tasks fall, of course, at the busiest and most stressful time for top managers. Still, communication is key, and it must not be neglected.

Ten Critical Questions—Filing Chapter 11 Business Reorganization

10. What happens if the case fails?

A large majority of Chapter 11 cases are converted to Chapter 7 for liquidation or are dismissed. Others, when true reorganization cannot be accomplished, turn to Chapter 11 Plans of Liquidation. As a result of this action, the company is liquidated (which technically is a form of "reorganization") and the proceeds are paid to the creditors. In many such cases, the only creditor to receive anything is the secured creditor with a lien on assets. These creditors frequently are paid less than full value on their claims, even when all assets are liquidated for their benefit.

The low success rates for Chapter 11 cases are attributable, in part, to cases which never had a real chance in Chapter 11 because they were too poorly capitalized, too poorly managed, left behind by technological change, or headed by inexperienced managers or lawyers. Success requires realism, resilience, and rigorous planning and preparation. Contingency planning and flexibility are also required. Capable and experienced counsel is critical to success.

As in all fields of human endeavor, fear of failure must not be allowed to predominate the effort. Chapter 11 reorganization is one of many complex business maneuvers which can be executed by competent and dedicated managers. To be successful, the plan must be executed correctly. And it will only succeed under the right circumstances. Failure of a reorganization should not be considered to be a badge of shame or a sign of weakness. And, when plans are confirmed and reorganization is achieved, the "save" is truly a remarkable accomplishment.

Index

341 Meeting 25-27, 59
363 Sale 37-38
2004 Exam 27-28
9019 Motion 27, 51-53

A

adversary proceeding 12, 28, 50-52
assets, sales of 37, 87
assets, schedules of 23
automatic stay 6, 10-11, 58-59
avoidance 6, 22, 29-33, 50-51, 64, 69

B

bankruptcy, involuntary 54-55
bankruptcy, personal 78-86, 93

C

cash collateral 39, 91
Chapter 7 .... 3, 6, 8, 14-16, 47, 56-58, 62, 84-85
Chapter 9 3-4
Chapter 11 .... 4-5, 22, 25-27, 34, 37-40, 47-49, 60-65, 87-98
Chapter 12 5
Chapter 13 .... 3, 5-6, 56, 84-85
claim, proof of 21-23
compromise 14, 52, 57
contract 2, 10, 13, 41-43
credit card 56, 76, 82, 85
creditors, meeting of 25, 26, 34, 59

D

debtor in possession 31, 34, 40, 50, 62, 64, 91, 92
debts, schedules of 37, 87
DIP financing 40, 91, 92
discharge 1, 3-11, 17, 18, 42, 47, 50, 51, 54, 57, 65
divorce 1, 32, 71, 72, 79, 80

E

eviction 58
exemption 14-20, 57-58

F

fraudulent conveyance 29-33, 37-38, 55, 69, 71

Index

I
involuntary bankruptcy 54-55

L
landlord 58, 60
leases 10, 41-43, 60, 88
lien 3, 10-17, 22, 30, 32, 33, 35, 37, 39, 40, 55, 64
liquidation 3, 6, 8, 14, 16, 37, 49, 66, 87, 94, 98
luxury goods 8, 9, 57, 76

M
means test 56, 66, 84, 85
meeting of creditors 25, 26, 34, 59
mortgage 12, 15, 16, 39, 55, 68

N
non-dischargeable 8, 9, 57

P
personal bankruptcy 78-86, 93
preferences 29-31, 50, 55
proof of claim 21-23
priority claim 22, 60, 62, 65, 93
property rights 11

R
reaffirmation 17, 42, 58, 73
real estate 5, 15, 41, 47, 66-69, 83
reorganization 4, 5, 9, 11, 22, 24, 25, 28, 36, 38,
41, 42, 47, 49, 50, 61, 87-98
residency requirement 15, 58
retirement 8, 19, 20, 57, 58, 74, 83, 84, 89

S
sales of assets 37, 87
schedules of debts and assets 23
stay, automatic 6, 10-11, 58-59

U
U.S. Trustee 23, 25, 34, 35, 45, 92

The minute you read something and you can't understand it, you can almost be sure it was drawn up by a lawyer. Then, if you give it to another lawyer and he don't know just what it means, why then you can be sure it was drawn up by a lawyer.

Will Rogers

Appellate Judge Mark Painter is on a mission to eliminate "legal-ese" from the legal landscape. Over the years, he has taught dozens of CLE seminars devoted to simplifying legal writing.

Judge Painter's book, *The Legal Writer*, is written to enlighten lawyers, judges, paralegals, and just about anyone who writes to persuade.

Judge Painter has constructed 40 simple, yet effective rules to guide writers through errors commonly made by legal professionals. The 168-page book also identifies court citation styles and contact information for the Supreme Courts of all 50 states.

And it is now available through Casemaker® Print Publishing for only $26.95 plus shipping and handling.

For this and other new print releases, visit our website at:
www.casemaker.cc

Or send a check or money order for $31.45 to:
Lawriter Corporation
250 East Fifth Street
Suite 444
Cincinnati, OH 45202